Praise for *Playing the Matrix*

"Thank you for the perspective on what desire is and how it serves us.
The clarity on ways to play the game of life is genius—and so practical!"

"My son and I attended your seminar in Philadelphia this past weekend.
I cannot begin to tell you the effect you have made on him (and me)."

"You explain the questions I have grappled with all my life—
but you explain the core wrenching, serious answers so the listener
hears it with love, joy, and a sense of readiness to move forward."

"You brought amazing clarity to the manifestation process,
dispelled the fears I had around it, and greatly
empowered me to create the life of my dreams."

"I learned that I was focused on the wrong side of the Matrix and that
there's nothing wrong with me, just my lack of focus on my priorities."

"I see God's presence in you shining *so* brightly,
it helps me to shine even more."

"I have felt *stuck* for so long. Learning that the trick to manifesting my
dream life is to focus on the general idea of what I want and let the
Universe take care of everything else is *so* freeing!"

"I've struggled with the 'what do I want to do when I grow up'
issue and wrestled with 'what do I do next.' I finally feel clear on both
of these for the first time in years! I also feel like I 'get' the law of
attraction for the first time, how to apply it to my life, both in a big
picture way and in a 'what I'm going to do tomorrow' way."

"*The Secret* was the first step. Mike went deeper
and actually told us how to do it!"

"The biggest boost I got from your seminar was to focus
on *the end result* . . . It's been more powerful than I can explain.
And everyone I share it with seems to 'get it' very quickly.
Thank you for making it easy and profound."

"It's so good to hear all things are possible
and leave with the strategies to make them happen."

"Mike is an inspiration to everyone who has ever doubted their value. His perseverance, his action, his commitment to sharing the message is a gift. His playful delivery makes it fun."

"Mike's enthusiasm will inspire you, his energy will galvanize you, his honesty will comfort you and convince you to keep going! I always get a bit worried when I read testimonials that say things like 'awesome!' and 'the best workshop I have ever attended!' Seriously?! However . . . awesome! The best workshop I have ever attended! Thank you."

"An absolute 'must' for anyone wanting to change their life for the better."

"Mike Dooley's Matrix is one of the greatest guidelines to fulfilling your dreams and making them come true!"

"Mike makes it so easy to understand the Matrix . . . wouldn't it be great if *this* was taught in all of our schools?"

"One of the best workshops I've attended—offering practical, useable, easily implemented info that I can start using now!"

"I am so grateful. I loved it. I needed it. Thank you for reminding me of my power and showing me the tools."

"If only the world could all—every person—connect with this information!"

"Thank you! I am an engineer and I think in terms of formulas. Mike spoke to me in a manner that resonated—he gave me the formula and structure to help me to regain my power."

"This workshop totally shifted my understanding of goal setting."

"I was reading my workshop notes and handouts on the flight and it hit me again—the perfection of life as it is. I was crying again and smiling again and was just overwhelmed with happiness! Thank you, thank you, thank you . . ."

"I wouldn't have believed I'd find it so valuable—originally came only as part of a birthday present to my girlfriend."

"This was a highlight of my LIFE. Thanks so much!"

"I expected the program to be good, but it was above and beyond anything I ever imagined."

Playing the Matrix

ALSO BY MIKE DOOLEY

BOOKS

*From Deep Space with Love: A Conversation about Consciousness,
the Universe, and Building a Better World* (with Tracy Farquhar)*

*Life on Earth: Understanding Who We Are,
How We Got Here, and What May Lie Ahead**

*The Top 10 Things Dead People Want to Tell YOU**

Leveraging the Universe: 7 Steps to Engaging Life's Magic

Manifesting Change: It Couldn't Be Easier

Infinite Possibilities: The Art of Living Your Dreams

Choose Them Wisely: Thoughts Become Things!

Notes from the Universe: New Perspectives from an Old Friend

More Notes from the Universe: Life, Dreams and Happiness

Even More Notes from the Universe: Dancing Life's Dance

Notes from the Universe Coloring Book: Enjoy the Journey

An Adventurer's Guide to the Jungles of Time and Space
(formerly titled *Lost in Space*)

Totally Unique Thoughts: Reminders of Life's Everyday Magic

CARD DECKS

Notes from the Universe
Notes from the Universe on Abundance

DVDS

The Path Less Traveled: Performing Miracles
Manifesting Change: It Couldn't Be Easier
Thoughts Become Things

VIDEO COURSES

Love Your Life in 30 Days
*Playing the Matrix and Getting What You Really Want**
*A Trainer's Guide to Infinite Possibilities**

FOR CHILDREN

Your Magical Life
Dreams Come True: All They Need Is You

*Available from Hay House
Please visit:

Hay House USA: www.hayhouse.com®
Hay House Australia: www.hayhouse.com.au
Hay House UK: www.hayhouse.co.uk
Hay House South Africa: www.hayhouse.co.za
Hay House India: www.hayhouse.co.in

Playing
the
Matrix

A Program for Living Deliberately
and Creating Consciously

Mike Dooley

HAY
HOUSE

HAY HOUSE, INC.
Carlsbad, California • New York City
London • Sydney • Johannesburg
Vancouver • New Delhi

Cataloging-in-Publication Data is on file at the Library of Congress

Hardcover ISBN: 978-1-4019-5060-6

10 9 8 7 6 5 4 3 2 1
1st edition, October 2017

Printed in the United States of America

To my wife and daughter;
my joy and laughter.

CONTENTS

A Note from the Universe

Remember when, as a child, just the sight of a swing set, or a pony, or a Hula-Hoop would get your heart racing and your imagination somersaulting?

And without even thinking in words you felt that surely the world revolved around you, that you were the most blessed creature ever to live, and that having fun was all that really mattered?

Well, I still wonder how you knew so much, at such a tender age.

Tallyho,

The Universe

P.S. To me, at times, it's as if there is only you.
Actually . . . all the time.

INTRODUCTION

If you want happiness for an hour, take a nap. If you want happiness for a day, go fishing. If you want happiness for a year, inherit a fortune. If you want happiness for a lifetime, help somebody.

— CHINESE PROVERB

Seventeen years ago, months shy of turning a very scary "four oh!," at the lowest ebb of my life—distraught over a bad breakup, second career up in smoke, debt far exceeding life's savings—heartbroken, I wondered if I'd ever be happy again. By any account, my life was a train wreck.

Among other seemingly futile attempts to "get my groove back," I began sending out free inspirational e-mails, spiritual not religious, to visitors of our by-then-liquidated family retail T-shirt stores when they signed our guest books. And slowly—very slowly—I felt better.

Within a year, as my little mission grew and my website expanded with more "reminders of life's everyday magic," I found myself experiencing sporadic happiness. Within two, I was dating, earning, and had an impressive Internet following. After three, I began to regularly travel the world, really, the entire world, either bringing crowds with me or assembling locals where I landed, to share the truth about life's beauty and our power. Teaching that anyone, anywhere, no matter where they've been, no matter where they are, can learn how to live deliberately, create consciously, loved and in love. And on one such trip, even after I thought "it" might be too late for myself, I met a woman who'd later make me a first-time husband and father.

"Stranger than fiction," as they say.

YOU TEACH BEST WHAT YOU MOST NEED TO LEARN

I attribute my rather stunning rebound and ascent to the profound dynamic nailed by Richard Bach when he wrote, "You teach best what you most need to learn." In the midst of my recovery, indirectly and almost unintentionally, I began helping others as I endeavored to save myself, teaching what I most needed to learn—not only about how to salvage an upended life, but to rebound, blast off, and soar. Or, more eloquently, as the subtitle of my first audio program promised, I began teaching "the art of living your dreams."

Today, after all these years as my own student and instructor, through four world tours, speaking in 132 cities, between 34 countries, on six continents, my ultimate daylong presentation has evolved into Playing the Matrix. In it, I share all that I've learned, plus, with the benefit of hindsight, tell exactly what I did to unwittingly hasten a comeback that would wildly exceed my earlier life successes. It's become my most advanced program, not because it's complicated— it's not—but because it's so unconventional, unexpected, and at first, seemingly contradictory to all the wisdom taught by others. Some attendees have claimed their time at this event amounted to the best day of their lives, so far. They've been among mine, too.

While I've learned "what I most needed to learn" through teaching it, every step of the way I had to apply it, to walk the talk, and now, the biggest surprise, after seeing my own life so radically transformed, is finding how many other people I've helped. Tens of thousands of e-mails from fans—salt of the earth, clergy, and celebrities alike—have filled my in-box with notes of gratitude for what I've shared and the difference it's made in their lives. And as my life's "needs" have so clearly been met, materially and spiritually, ironically what I most care about is helping others help themselves; what began as the incidental by-product of saving *my* life, helping others, has come full circle to be my highest ambition—helping others. Who'd have thunk?

> **Life is not something that happens to you. You happen to life.**
> *You came first.*

PLAYING THE MATRIX

At the heart of this program is a simple concept for creating major life changes and living deliberately. It explains why "manifesting" sometimes works with incredible ease, why at other times it's painfully slow, and why at times it works, yet with hindsight we wish it hadn't! Among its many attributes, the Matrix helps practitioners navigate around dreams that lie within the Bermuda Triangle of Manifesting (to be explained herein), as well as untangling themselves from what are likely the three trickiest areas of intentional creation, by showing them how to:

1. Avoid self-sabotage through achieving greater clarity

2. Arouse the critical element of passion without attaching to unimportant details

3. Act on their dreams without "messing with the cursed hows"!

The Matrix also reveals the interconnectedness of our many dreams, and when "played properly" you'll see how they can add to one another, rather than negate one another. The resulting confluence of multiple, complementary dreams then creates a compounding effect that will bring you the greatest happiness and fastest breakthroughs.

In its purest essence, the Matrix is a tool for getting clear on what it is you really want, your desired end results, defined in a way that avoids contradictions and detours, more quickly availing you of life's magic, instead of setting you up for disappointments or, at best, occasional successes.

If "occasional" is no longer good enough, I have some great news. "All the time," however seemingly implausible, now lies within reach.

THE PREMISE

You're not here, in these hallowed jungles of time and space, by accident.

You're here because you chose to be here.

And you chose to be here for a reason. Many reasons. Not the least of which is to begin living your life deliberately, as you've always suspected you could. Alive in a paradise, cloaked in the illusion of matter, to discover that you truly have been given dominion over all things.

Life is not something that happens to you. You happen to life. *You came first.* You're the very reason the sun came up this morning. And even as you read these words, all the elements are looking to you for direction. Because you are, we all are, literally, the eyes and the ears of God almighty come alive in the dream of life. Your wish, therefore, is the entire Universe's command.

It's just that rarely, if ever, have you been taught the truth of your unimaginable power. Fortunately, however, not being told the truth has never stopped it from being true. In fact, throughout your entire life, using your thoughts, your words, and your actions, you've always been and you will always be a natural-born creator.

Distilled even further, this book will give you a better understanding of who you are, how you got here, and, above all, what you can still do with your time in space.

COME WITH ME

In the pages that follow, as in my daylong events, I'll immerse you in more of life's absolute, objective, immovable truths, which form the bedrock of a life to be lived in confidence, optimism, and great expectation. I'll share the actual physical and metaphysical mechanics of every earthly manifestation, including your role in the process, so that you can deliberately orchestrate the changes and transformation you most wish to see.

I will strive to convince you of your power, your worth, and how easy life can be once you begin working with the Universe instead of unwittingly working against it. You'll be given new tools and techniques that will help you turn theory into action, affording you the traction necessary to begin living the life you've always dreamed would be yours. After all, if I could do it, so can you . . . and so can anyone else.

Your great admirer,

Neil

Chapter 1

UNDERSTANDING "MIRACLES"

A Note from the Universe

Possessing the audacity to do the mundane, while expecting miracles to come from it, explains every heroic and supernatural feat known to humankind.

Audaciously,
The Universe

It's long been said, "It's not magic to the magician." To magicians, their routines are both "easy" and "obvious," not magic. Why? Because they know what's going on. They've practiced. They take nothing for granted. Whereas the observer, the audience, has no idea of what's about to happen, is inexperienced in "magic," and takes everything for granted.

In the jungles of time and space, who's the magician of your life? You are. Who's the observer, the most important "audience member"? You're both. Yet, because you misunderstand the logistics of creation, your role in it, and how circumstances are forged, there's been a disconnect in which you've relegated yourself to mere witness and accidental bystander. As if life was indifferent to your presence! Failing to see how profoundly integral you are,

1

breathing life into everything you experience to a degree hereto-fore unimaginable.

Yet with closer inspection and a little practice, you're about to discover the truth. That not only is life miraculous, 24/7, but that in yours, you're its conductor. Meaning, of course, given how the world now defines a miracle, as extremely unusual, beyond human control, of a divine intervention, there's no such thing! Ergo, the day is fast approaching when, as magicians feel about magic, people will no longer see miracles as miracles, but as easy, obvious, ordinary, natural, and probably, to be fair, cool.

The massive extent of what we presently take for granted was captured by the late Carl Sagan, famed scientist and astronomer, who wrote the book *Contact* that later became a movie starring Jodie Foster.

"If you wish to make an apple pie from scratch . . .
you must first invent the universe."

Typically, we think scratch means, what? Organic apples from a farmer's market, right? Skipping over the fact that to have an apple you've got to have an apple tree, which requires the right conditions, in the right season, at the right age. Further taking for granted that this tree needs a planet exactly as old as ours is, exactly the size ours is, exactly the distance ours is from a sun exactly the size and age ours is. Not to mention all the symbiotic relationships, between birds and bees and things that makes apple trees flourish, grow, and propagate. There's so much more neces-sary to have a mere, lone apple, it would take more words than are in this entire book to do the job—before even getting to the pie crust! All of which is given to us, as if miraculously, without any effort.

Now think about this: You start sentences you don't know how you'll complete, yet they usually make sense. You beat your heart almost 5,000 times per hour without a thought. You're replacing cells in your body that are expiring this moment with new cells in the exact right places—toe cells in your toes, nose cells in your nose, thankfully. And right now, while beating your heart and replacing cells, you're reading! You can probably walk across a room, chew gum, digest food, and hum to yourself, all at the same time, while averting chaos and disaster. Masterful. You see with your eyes, hear with your ears, smell with your nose, feel with your skin, and think with your mind, yet here's the rub: You have absolutely no idea how you really do any of these things! You perform magic and miracles, day in and day out, without notice or thought. And of course, as you'll read in the course of this book, your miracles extend far beyond your body's involuntary system and talking to include orchestrating the very logistics of your every waking moment—such as manifesting parking spaces, finding travel partners, healing, and the creation of financial wealth, or not, for starters. These things *you* already ordain.

A HINT ON HOW WE PERFORM "MIRACLES"

Taking less for granted and paying closer attention, perhaps we can see what's happening in the case of our more conscious miracles, like walking, for example:

To Perform Miracles:

1. Possess intention to achieve desired end result, and,

2. Humbly, if naively, physically move in the desired direction.

After which your glorious body, subconscious, so-called involuntary system, or "life's everyday magic," call it what you will, does the rest.

We take a lot for granted, don't we? In fact, we're really good at it. And very likely, their performance isn't supposed to occupy brain bandwidth, so that we can get on with our lives, or perish. But what if you at least gave yourself credit for all you do and how you really do it? After all, it's undeniably you, performing the seeming impossible 24/7, year-round, lifelong. Maybe the trick to getting "miracles" lies in understanding that you're already performing them?

And here's another irony: For the complicated stuff like replacing toe cells with toe cells, walking, talking, and sitting upright to read a book, you have no problem with "delegating" or relying on life's everyday magic (again, whatever you call it, but I'll simply use life's magic through the rest of this book). But for the easy, simple, baby-cake stuff, that the Universe would love to knock out of the park for you, like, losing weight, paying off bills, surrounding yourself with friends and laugher, and finding a job you don't think of as work, you're like, "Oh no, it's all on me. How am *I* going to do that? I'll need more willpower, coaches, love, help, courage, therapy, and maybe a past-life regression to rid myself of twelfth-century karma. I better attend more seminars, watch more DVDs, and read more books."

> Maybe the trick to getting "miracles" lies in understanding that you're already performing them?

Not after this one.

Instead, all you really need to do is begin delegating the easy stuff to life's magic, too. Again, it's simply a matter of intention, an imagined end result that aligns your circuitry and sets gears into motion, so that you might even brush your hair, for example. Easy. Just as you're doing it now, assimilating meaning from these words. Why not let life's magic help you pay off bills, improve your health, live pain free, find that person who completes you or a career that's an absolute joy? The Universe is like, "I'm all over it! Let me at it!" But you've gotten in your own way, and therefore in its way, by thinking that you're alone.

No more.

Over the years within my workshops, I've contrived numerous analogies and metaphors to help students "get out of their own way," emphasizing they needn't manipulate physical circumstances, or people, to achieve their desired dreams. One of my favorites, that's not yet made its way into a book, comes from comparing our nighttime dreams to the waking dream of life.

A Note from the Universe

The reason most people don't see miracles is because there's just so bloomin' many of them.

Like this very moment . . .

And this one . . .

And this one . . .

Ah-h-h-h,
The Universe

WHEN A DREAM IS NOT A DREAM

Aren't the dreams we have at night cool? The coolest thing about nighttime dreams is that anything can happen. You don't have a nighttime dream where you're surrounded by laughter and friends and abundance one night, and then say, "Stop, stop, this makes no sense, I was poor and alone in my last dream." *Anything can happen* in a nighttime dream, and what I want you to begin seeing is that although things are a bit less flexible and more time is needed to create change, the same is true of the "waking dream" we now share.

Let's be sure we're on the same page when it comes to what a *nighttime* dream is:

- Who creates our nighttime dreams? *We do.* A psychiatrist would tell you that, a medical doctor would tell you that, a hippie would tell you that. Everyone would agree we create our own nighttime dreams.

- What are our dreams made of? Are they brick and mortar? Of course not. They're made of *thought*. Wispy, intangible thoughts.

- And a redundant question, but the third and final one to make sure we're on the same page: *Whose* thoughts are our dreams at night? *Ours.* Our dreams are our own. They're made of thought. They're made of *our thoughts.*

Now I'd like to share with you a recurring dream experience that I had for decades beginning from the time I was about 18. In these nighttime dreams, all of a sudden mid-dream it would dawn on me that I was dreaming. I'd think to myself, *This must be a dream, it makes no sense at all how I could be here; I remember nothing leading up to this scene . . . but now I'm here and it's as real as can be . . . it must be a dream!* I'd get really excited within the dream . . . *I'm waking up inside my dream; this is a lucid dream! It's all mine . . . I want to go do stuff, break physical laws, fly, be crazy!* But first, I *had to* make sure it really was a dream so that I wouldn't get in trouble, or break any bones! I'd look around, not sure of what I was look-ing for, maybe something to convince me it was really a dream. What would *you* look for to see whether it was a dream? Duct tape? A tear in the sky? Some weird un-filled-in space? Usually I'd be dreaming I was outdoors, so I'd look up at the sky, and there it was, the wild blue yonder . . . and I'd think to myself, *Wow, that looks so real . . .* And as I'd be looking at the beautiful blue sky, I'd see off in the distance a couple of puffy white clouds slowly floating along. And as I'd be gazing at the clouds, I'd notice a flock of seagulls that would appear to the right and fly all the way across the sky. And I'd think, *Dang, that's gotta be real, maybe this isn't a dream . . .* But I wasn't going to give up that easily, so I'd look over to where there was a stand of trees, and I'd scrutinize them to the point of seeing every imaginable shade of green as the sun danced on the leaves that were being blown by the breeze, and again I'd think, *That's so real; this can't a dream!* I'd look beneath my feet and stomp on the firm earth. I'd even pinch myself and it would hurt.

Each time I had this dream, I ended up drawing the same conclusion: *This* can't *be a dream; it's much, much too real!* And then sometime later the alarm clock would go off, I'd wake up groggy, searching for my bearings, recall the dream, and think, *It* was *a dream, IT WAS! And I WAS waking up in the middle of it . . . but not believing what I thought to be true . . . I lost my grip and slipped back into being the unknowing dreamer . . . DANG!* Years would go by and then I'd have the exact same experience followed by the exact same conclusions and the exact same disappointment when I woke up, so I began asking, "Why? What am I supposed to do in these dreams? What am I supposed to do when I finally wake up and realize it's a dream?" When, over many years, I didn't get an answer to these questions, one day I thought to change the question to, "What is this telling me?" And *immediately* three epiphanies came to mind, two of which are easy as pie. The third is a doozy and will require you find a safe zone to process. Please turn off any heavy machinery.

> It's one kind of victory to slay a beast, move a mountain, and cross a chasm, but it's another kind altogether to realize that the beast, the mountain, and the chasm were of your own design.

The First Epiphany

The dreams we have when we sleep are real. Every bit as real as waking life. It's just that our memory of them seems foggy because we don't normally have the conscious wherewithal to scrutinize our nighttime dreams. Normally, we just run from the monster, have our arguments, or do whatever we find ourselves doing, without the scrutiny that I had the benefit of as I awoke within my dream. Which is actually something our nighttime dreams have in common with our waking dreams: We don't usually scrutinize the props in our lives. Do you know how many lamps are above your head right now? Or what color the floor is beneath your feet? Do you even remember the color of the socks or the underwear you're wearing right now? We usually think our dreams are nebulous and hazy, right? We remember the feelings we had, but our recollection of the props is foggy . . . *similar to how yesterday looks to us today!* No doubt, if you had thought to question things yesterday, what you now think of as foggy would have been crystal clear! And so, I'm proposing that our nighttime dreams are exactly as real as our waking life.

The Second Epiphany

The waking dream that we're sharing now is every bit as illusionary, as wispy, as our nighttime dreams. This is encouraging because if there's a mountain in your life, or lions and tigers and bears, it's easier to contend with such when you realize that they're not as immovable as you once thought they were; they are, in part, a product of your perceptions. It's one kind of victory to slay a beast, move a mountain, and cross a chasm, but it's another kind altogether to realize that the beast, the mountain, and the chasm were of your own design!

A Note from the Universe

When I survey life's majesty: the birds, the bees, and the African tulip trees. And when I survey life's characters: the Abdullahs, the Lilis, and the Kaylas. And when I consider life's tribulations: the setbacks, the losses, the fear. And when I consider life's abundance, its glories, its order. And when I . . . actually, I could go on forever . . . literally.

Do you know what I love the most?

How real it all seems.

> *Nothing is,*
> *The Universe*

The Third Epiphany

Brace yourself.

To revisit the question of who creates our dreams at night: *You* would tell *me* that when I looked into the wild blue yonder of my nighttime dream (which presumably appeared blue because of sunlight passing through the atmosphere); when I saw puffy white clouds (presumably the result of a warming earth and the condensation of rising, humid air reaching cooler altitudes); and when I saw the flock of seagulls crossing the sky (because they know how to gain lift and fly), you would tell me that *I* created all that I saw, right? Right!? My dreams are my thoughts are my creations. Yes? And my former self would have probably replied to you, "No way, get out of here; I was *experiencing* all of that; I didn't know there'd be clouds or seagulls up there until I looked and happened to see them. Besides, I have no idea what makes the sky so blue." And you'd say, "No, dude, you created that," and I'd say, "No, I experienced it; I was there witnessing it, not creating it."

> Any desired end result held in our minds will strive to force the physical details, laws, and circumstances necessary for it to emerge into our life.

See where this is going?

Streaming Manifestors

In our nighttime dreams, all of us are streaming manifestors. We're creating, and streaming into place, not just the players we meet in our dreams, but the entire dream bubble, including the gravity that holds our dreaming feet in place, as well as all other relevant physical laws! How do we do this? No doubt it's through belief, intent, expectation, and desire, but it really doesn't matter, does it? What matters is that the bubble is created (or that this Matrix exists, like in the movie except with no malevolence) so that in it you can play out your lessons or achieve whatever the purpose of the dream was.

You've heard the expression "streaming music, streaming audio, streaming video" on the Internet, right? If you have a media player on your laptop or smartphone and you're streaming a movie or a song, you can grab the little scroll bar, click and drag it, left or right, and suddenly you're moving into the past or the future of the movie or song. In other words, *what wasn't being experienced a second ago is now there in all its glory.* You command, through sliding the scroll bar, where you'll begin experiencing what already exists in your download or your stream. Yes?

At night when we dream, we stream. We put it there. Instantaneously. Whatever we need on the stage of our dream is projected automatically *by us.* Unlike Internet entertainment, obviously, what you stream is not predetermined, but exactly like Internet entertainment, you get to choose where your focus is. Best part: *You don't have to know how you do it to realize you're doing it* (as we've shown), and once you realize you're doing it you can start asking the question, "What else could I stream?"

A very logical answer to this new question presents itself: *whatever you want, within the loose confines of the dream.*

Now, the million-dollar question, "Why do you think we hide from ourselves, within our nighttime dreams, the fact that we're streaming it all into place?" This is huge. Why do we hide from ourselves that we're creating our dream experience as we're experiencing it?

There's a logical answer to this, too: So that it can seem *real,* or to maybe use a less confusing word, so that it can seem *believable!* Authentic! Happening! *Something you must deal with!*

If what's happening seems real, then and only then can there be adventure. Then and only then can you fleetingly believe in have versus have not, here versus there, now versus then. Stuff that is otherwise pure illusion. If you knew you were streaming it all, it would be boring, but by fleetingly (for the duration of a nighttime dream, or a waking lifetime) believing that the illusions are reality, you are gripped by your passions, scared by your fears, and thrown into action! Lights! Camera! Go! Your life takes form . . . Journeys unfold as you pursue whatever happiness means to you—the whole, entire point of being alive in the jungles of time and space!

When you start to get this, you can start deliberately poking around "the backlot" of your mind, dabbling with your focus and choosing your thoughts. You start to understand the meaning behind the words, *thoughts become things.* They literally do! How? *Doesn't matter!* They do! We can see that this is true in our night-time dreams, just as we begin to know it must be happening in our daytime lives. We don't have to worry about the logistics. Those are the "hows," which will be taken care of for us as surely as our hearts keep beating. Any desired end result held in our minds, in our thoughts, will strive to force the physical details, laws, and circumstances necessary for it to ultimately emerge, manifested, into our life.

To be clear, I'm not speaking about nighttime dreams to explore *why* we have them. That's a different subject. I'm speaking about the logistics and the realization that you project it all into place as a nonstop streamer. When you understand this, you realize your astounding powers of matter manipulation and you can start the magnificent work of *deliberately* changing the scenery of your life.

To Paint an Even Clearer Picture

Diving deeper into nighttime dreams, here's how they unfold and how you stream. Does the set presumably call for a cottage on the beach, "blink," you've got a cottage on the beach. You could go to your dreamed-of cottage and rub the exterior walls, look at your hand, and see the oxidized paint because it hasn't been painted in 12 years. You might think, *Now wait a minute. This is a dream and there was nothing there a blink ago, yet now the whole stage is set with physical laws, a past, and a history, all combined!* In the instant you "blink" to a *cottage at the beach* in a nighttime dream, everything is taken care of for you. Look down at your feet and just like a flashlight in the dark *your consciousness* will project a million grains of sand. You can look out at "the ocean," and while nothing was there a moment ago, now you have a sea that's millions of years old.

If your dream calls for a house, in a forest, in Vermont, presto, you'll be at that home, but rather than going in through the front door, you can walk around to the back, and where there was nothing moments ago, suddenly you have woods: little seedlings that sprang last spring, baby trees, and 12 paces away a mighty oak that's 150 years old. Not far from it, there's the tree that blew down in last fall's storm, and beyond that there's another downed oak that fell many years ago, still in the process of decay . . . *and a second ago nothing was there.* Yet, it's all there now because *you are there*, projecting it into place! It's all illusions! Real illusions, at least to the "you" in the dream!

> Which means, you are a matter manipulator, a natural born creator, a miracle worker who so far has not given yourself the credit you deserve!

This is what you do every single night when you have a nighttime dream. And again, the point of all this is to suggest that the nighttime dream *is no different from the waking dream of here and now.* Have you heard the rhetorical question that asks: When a tree falls in the woods and no one's there to hear it, does it make a sound? Now you know the answer: If there's no one there, there's no woods, and no tree! It only exists when we go there and we stream it into place. This is where the Matrix, *from the movie*, makes sense, as it theoretically holds everything together, past, present, and future, among an infinite number of probable timelines, and within each there's the space for evolution, the passage of time, and physical laws, which, however, are only made manifest if someone later shows up at their "coordinate points" through a focus on said time, space, or matter.

If you were having a nighttime dream right now, what would be on the other side of the ceiling or the nearest wall of the room you had dreamed into place? Void, right? Nothing, because you're having a dream, so there'd be nothing beyond your needs. Well, right now in the dream of here and now, what do you think is on the other side of the walls holding up the room you now find yourself in? *Nothing until you, or somebody, goes there and streams it into place.* Of course, in the dream of life there's continuity, presumably made possible by an energy matrix or grid and time-space coordinate points, ensuring that your car will remain where you parked it, and others can find it there, even though no one may have been near it to stream it in your absence. Which we'll touch on next. Nevertheless, we're still able to sense the astounding nature of a life lived within the illusions where we're streaming everything we experience every single day. Which means you are a natural born creator, a miracle worker who so far has not given yourself the credit you deserve!

The Difference between Waking and Sleeping Dreams

There are two "little" differences between our nighttime dream bubbles and the matrix of here and now.

1. The first is continuity: In the dream of here and now, there is continuity of time, space, matter, and our own evolving thoughts and beliefs. This is very handy as just illustrated, as it means your car, and your car keys, will be wherever you left them. Continuity is also important in the sense that your dreams can now last an entire lifetime with lots of love, adventure, learning, and growth instead of 20 minutes or 20 seconds like in a nighttime dream. It's also handy in that it means the Eiffel Tower will stay in Paris and we can all use it as a reference point.

   This also introduces a new element worth noting concerning affecting change in the dream of life. In the nighttime dream you can think of the Eiffel Tower and "blink," you're there on the Champs-Elysées. All the details are forced, streamed, in order for the dream to make sense. There are to-ers and fro-ers, people walking, coming and going. Here in the dream of life, however, if you think of the Eiffel Tower, there's something else that must be added to the equation for you to stream it into place. What do you now have to do in time and space if you want to experience the Eiffel Tower as reality? *You have to physically go there, because of this continuity.* Blinking is not enough. You have to take action. It's still a dream. You're still projecting it in a streaming fashion, but to give yourself permission to do that in a believable, real way, you have to *physically* take action. Buy the ticket, get to the airport, fly on the plane, and clear immigration. It's not an option. You have to move. And when you move, the Universe moves. Action is how you navigate in the continuity soup of the here and now.

2. The second difference between our nighttime dream and our waking dream is that we're sharing our waking dream with 7.5 billion co-dreamers, each of us on a holy pilgrimage to discover life's beauty and our own powers, which means that each of us is untouchable by the others unless they have our consent (no matter how much it may seem otherwise). Which means that if you want to create change among the players of your life, you have to do something that you don't have to do in a nighttime dream (and it's the same thing you did to get to Charles de Gaulle Airport): You have to physically take action. You have to do something. It's still a dream, and it's still being streamed, but if you want a new travel partner, new friends, new clients, new customers, you have to physically do something in order for everything else to move about the set— sign up at Match.com, go to a bowling alley, hang out at the mall, mingle with co-workers, shake new hands, network, make cold calls. Then you'll have permission to bring new people into your life, while distancing yourself from others. Like attracts like, and those people who have dreams complementary to those of your changing mind will then appear.

Takeaway: It's all illusions! Your life, your world, our world— 100 percent. Illusions that we create through focus. Our thoughts become things. How? *Forget the hows.* They're not important. Be concerned with the hows and you'll overthink and bog down. Instead, focus on what you want, think of it as done, imagine you are there. Happy, fulfilled, creative, and whatever else you want to be. Then, following your seemingly feeble baby steps, the world changes, at first imperceptibly, then, with consistence, gigantically. The illusions and circumstances of your life will be forced into place, as if magically and miraculously. You don't have to make the sky blue in your nighttime dreams, or in your daytime life. Similarly, you don't have to know where your soul mate is coming from, how you'll acquire financial abundance, heal from disease, or find work that's play. All physical details, laws, and serendipitous circumstances necessary for the streaming of your dream's manifestation are summoned and forced into place by our intentions and focus. Let these pieces of the puzzle effortlessly show up as you merely hold on to your vision and physically move in its direction, thereby navigating continuity, retaining authenticity, and creating space for the so-called accidents and coincidences that will lead to your own not-so-mysterious miracles.

THOUGHTS BECOME THINGS

As subjective as every life is and must be, it takes very little to see one objective pattern within all, to source our power and to begin applying it willfully: People get what they think about. The formula for creating change begins with *intent*. Your intent. Your chosen focus. Where you place your energy in formulating thoughts, words, and actions.

And wouldn't you fully expect this? That the propulsion of life, or our shared lives, would have to have a baseline and common thread? Something that ties everyone and everything together? That creates cohesion and continuity? That makes all things, new and old, possible? Yes? Obvious? A grid or matrix through which to play out our adventures with inviolate parameters, although very few, that gives us our tomorrows on much the same terms as we received them today? Indeed.

If we ask these questions, the answers appear. They're within us; our lives evidence them. But we haven't been taught to go within, we've been taught that the answers lie outside of us, with God, in books, anywhere but within. So rather than asking, people have believed what they were told, given the community or cultures they were born into. Some were told God is an angry man who put us here to test us, judge us, and sentence us. Others were taught that humanity must be the evolutionary by-product of single-cell oceanic organisms (with no theory on where they came from, much less the ocean and planets themselves) that replicated, sprung gills, and waddled out upon land, learning to walk upright . . . in high heels.

The idea that life and consciousness was bestowed on us by a God whose brilliance accounts for the entire universe—but possesses the emotional maturity of a 12-year-old—is shockingly illogical. Similarly, that life is the result of chance boggles the mind with contradictions and oversights; ignoring the elephant in the room: their implication that conscious evolved from matter!

How about this? Instead of trying to explain our origins, let's first just look at what is? What binds us? To what we all have in common? To what all our lives tell us? To why we breathe?

To be happy.

Can you think of a single objective in your life, or in the life of anyone, that doesn't directly or indirectly move you or them toward greater happiness? Happiness includes and implies our desire to survive, to love, and to be loved. It includes our selfless and altruistic urges for family, friends, and complete strangers. For example, you want your child to be happy not just for your child's happiness, *but for your own.* You may have a great many wishes that do not, at face value, have anything to do with your happiness, but for each of their outcomes, your happiness would ultimately be part of the equation.

Okay, then, let's ask how we can become so? The answer for one and all would be:

Our thoughts.

This is for the insights already shared and all that will follow. Moreover, right now we're establishing that we aren't necessarily here to learn *how* our thoughts become things, but perhaps, if we want to have more fun and be happier, to notice *that* they do. Not some of them, all of them. Not sometimes, all the time. Not just the positive ones, the other ones too.

This is not to be confused with saying you get what you *want*. You don't and won't. Instead, as we've already found, you get what you intend, *made clear by what you predominantly think about, speak about, and act on* (all of which are variations of thought and how it is expressed). You wanted it like this; for the dream of life to be a perfect reflection of all that dwelled within, even if you didn't know some of it dwelled within. What better way to find out than meeting it in the flesh! If only your fluffy, good thoughts became things, you'd never learn of your power or responsibilities. You wanted it all—including the lions, and tigers, and bears—so that you could overcome those that appeared by accepting the invitation inward they represented, asking you to patch up the confused or contradictory thinking that needed attention. Sound far-fetched? Well, if you really wish to effect change in your life, you must then ask: *What's the alternative?* To find your own way, or be buffeted about by a seemingly haphazard, irrational Universe.

A Note from the Universe

Only in hindsight will the miracles become obvious, will you see you were guided, and will you find there was order all along.

Something to remember,
The Universe

THE REAL SECRET

There really was a secret, not one that Leonardo da Vinci or Benjamin Franklin hid from their peers. That was marketing. The secret was, and in many cases still is, that humankind, all of us, men, women, and children, are natural born creators, *but no one has known it.* As a result, instead of deliberately creating, we've *reacted* to our creations without realizing that by focusing on "what is," we perpetuate it—good, bad, or ugly. This secret, that we are natural born creators for the thoughts we choose, explains why, since the beginning of time, there've been both men and women who have had a dream and the courage or naivety to move with it, radically improving their lives, raising the bar and setting a new standard of living for all to follow. It's also why, since the beginning of time, there have been men and women who have led lives filled with bitter disappointment, because they had no idea that by focusing on what was truly unjust and unfair, they were perpetuating its existence in their lives.

The Rich and Famous

The secret explains why Elon Musk, Lady Gaga, and Usain Bolt became household names the world over. They each had dreams and the nerve to think they could come true, and so they moved with their vision, their intention, which is all the Universe and life's magic needs to bring anyone's dream to pass. Have it, hold on to it, do something about it, and then your sails are hoisted to catch the magical winds of the Universe. Their end results were either 1) wild success or 2) bliss through following their hearts, and as they moved toward their dream, these things were pressed out to them through shifting and changing circumstances *ordained by their vision.* Always, our imagined end results force our life's circumstances to put us into a place of receivership.

> *The end in mind forces the details. Thought forces circumstance.*

It's not just for famous people. It works for everything. Money's pretty handy, and there are people of every race, every age, male, and female, who woke up one morning to discover they were millionaires. Their earlier end results, directly *or indirectly*, implied wild success financially, and as they humbly moved toward such, again, it was pressed to them through shifting and changing circumstances *ordained by their vision*. This is how it happens. It sneaks up on you. You don't actually go to sleep one night poor and wake up the next morning rich. You're active, you're busy, you're moving in the direction of your dreams, and suddenly you realize, *it happened to me*. It happens so often that it doesn't even make the news. If it happened to you in the next six months, your net worth suddenly in seven figures, your local media probably wouldn't even pick up the story because it's so common! Not that you even have to have that much money to live comfortably. But it's not just money, living deliberately and creating consciously works on *everything*.

The Salt of the Earth

Right now, in your immediate area, there are happy office workers; proud, beaming schoolteachers; gloating parents, who are rocking their lives *because they simply focus on what they love, and physically move with those thoughts*. They make the best of what's before them and the Universe is like, *I can play that game, more of what you love coming right up!*

You don't have to look far to see "the secret" in action. Listen to those in your home. Listen to your family, friends, and co-workers. Listen to the ones who say, "Life is hard. People are mean." The Universe hears every word we speak. Our words *are* our end results! These are the very people who can't seem to get a fair shake. And aren't those who claim to have no free time the ones who have no free time? Those who say *there are no good men, or women, available,* the ones who stay single? Who claim that life is a test, always being tested? Who think life's an adventure, always on an adventure? Eerie . . . or thoughts becoming things?!

The key is finally understanding the truth that has been staring us in the face since the dawn of time: understanding that our thoughts unfailingly become the things and events of our lives; understanding we don't have to know "how," we just have to know "what" it is we want. Understanding that we live in a dream world of illusions that bend, and move, and sway to whatever we think, speak, and move with.

The Greatest Secret of All Secrets

The greatest secret of all secrets is that all manifestations begin with the *end* in mind, in thought, including these very hallowed jungles themselves, time, space, and the physical (illusionary) universe with its estimated 10 sextillion stars. Divine Mind *imagined* the vastness, the beauty, symbiotic relationships, and Big Bang followed! In an instant, all the math and all the sciences and all the laws and properties necessary for life as we now know it came to be. And ever since then evolution took over, with some turtles growing longer necks, humans walking with straighter backs, and cheetahs running faster.

The answer to the creationism versus evolution conundrum, is "both," and probably more. I propose Big Bang was a form of the now-scoffed-at, archaic view of reality creation called spontaneous generation. I don't think a living organism ever sprang from nonliving matter, instead, through a mold made in Divine Mind, "outside" of time and space, of a desired outcome that would create a vehicle for the expression of life. And I propose that there have been similar instances of spontaneous generation following Big Bang that might, sometimes, explain the sudden discovery of new species. Yet these would be extremely rare, because today, as a rule, we're already under full sail, the game of our adventures is well underway, we've agreed to abide by the physical laws of the world, and evolution has emerged as the perceived and most believed-in way of bringing on change and transformation.

Whether this proposal is actually fact, I don't know. It doesn't matter! We can nevertheless see in our lives today that our thoughts, over time, held consistently, when acted upon, become the things and events we physically meet. What else matters? It's not the "hows" you're to be concerned with, but the "Wows!"—as long as there's understanding!

We can also see that today we enjoy the momentum (the continuity) of more than seven billion human co-creators, and those who came before us, of all that we share. Though pointedly and importantly, not with regard to the vast majority of your personal adventures; not with regard to your private abundance, joy, and health levels that remain for you to achieve. For these, you are their sole creator (talk about freedom!). In either case, however, to steer an evolution of circumstances and events that will bring your desires to pass, simply create a picture of your desired end result in your mind, do what you can to consistently move in its direction, which will permit a kind of slow and subtle metamorphosis of your life, vis-à-vis "coincidences and accidents," ultimately yielding a day that mirrors, physically, what you were first only thinking about.

This is how to use your brain. This is why you have it! Do you like what's going on in various areas of your life? "Yes." "Yes." "No." For any "no" area, the way to spark change is to create a new picture in your mind of what you want there, and then "show up." Your physical movement allows the Universe to move, dots are invisibly connected, and the next thing you know you're on life's yellow brick road, wondering, as I now do, *How did I ever get here? This is so awesome. My life is so sweet. What did I ever do to deserve so much?* Yet, really, I know, and so, soon, will you . . . we are natural born creators and our end results, in ways we cannot comprehend with our brains, forge new *circumstances*, stunning and seemingly miraculous, that will yield what we were after.

You've been doing this your entire life. The end in thought, in mind, forces the details and circumstances around you, putting you next to the right person, on the right plane, on the right day, who will give you an idea, leading you to act, drawing you, most unexpectedly, into a field of new friends and peers, and, hypothetically, as if further drawing from the ether whatever else you need, even self-confidence and creativity, to have, do, or be whatever you've been thinking about.

> **Through understanding "miracles," we realize that this system we're learning to play always works!**

The end in mind forces the details. Thought forces circumstance. You simply have to dream and show up. And perhaps, let's add, have faith. Because you pretty much don't get to see your progress until the entire process is complete, yet you must nevertheless hold on to the vision of your heart's desire, and continue to take action on it, however seemingly futile, with nothing to show for it, yet.

Digital GPS Navigation

To step this down and get you fully on board, I want to compare the stunning similarities between digital GPS navigation and the seemingly miraculous mechanics behind every manifestation.

Program Your Destination

What's the first thing that has to happen in your GPS-guided car for there to be a successful, happy adventure to a place you've never been before—synonymous with a dream coming true, of something happening in your life you've never experienced before? What's the first thing that has to happen, assuming engine is already idling, seat belt is fastened, and Barry Manilow is belting out "I Write the Songs"? You have to tell your GPS system your desired destination! And to use the terminology now appropriate for those who understand miracles, tell your system your desired "end result." Through GPS signals it already knows your starting point (like Divine Mind knows where you are in your life, second by second), so the instant you give the system your end result, working backward to where you now are, it then knows every possible road you could take. Speed limits and distances are compared. Traffic conditions and detours are weighed. Yields, merges, and traffic lights are factored. And presto, it knows the shortest, happiest way for you to arrive; it knows "how." Similar to all manifestation, *in GPS navigation your desired end result "forces" the path;* the details, circumstances, and logistics that will get you there from where you were, based upon the representation of the destination you at first only thought of. *The destination dictates how you're going to get there.* Right? But you're not there yet. You're still sitting in your parked car. What's the second thing you have to do for there to be an orderly and successful journey?

Put Your Car in Gear and Drive

The instant you give the system your end result, it knows how to get you there. It knows the best way. But if your car's in park, the entire system is designed *to not help you*. With your car in park, aren't you contradicting yourself? Isn't your inaction signaling, "Not yet! I'm not ready." Even if you didn't see the contradiction, you still are. If your car's in park, or if your life's in park as you, day in and day out, sit on the couch waiting for Oprah to call, you're simply not reachable, no matter how good the guidance is. And in your car, it won't matter if there's a vision board in the backseat. It won't matter if there's a gratitude rock in your pocket or purse. It won't matter if you're listening to my CDs. You won't be reachable by life's so-called accidents and coincidences that have a way of nudging you onto the right "roads."

In life, if you have a dream that thrills you, that you *don't* physically do something about, you short-circuit the so-called miracles. Too many spiritually aware people don't think they have to act "because the Universe loves me" and they've been taught that the Universe wants for them what they most want for themselves. True, true! But is wanting to drive to Miami enough to get there? Is wanting to live in financial abundance enough to have it delivered to your front door like a pizza? Never.

You can't be helped until you help yourself. And then your tiny efforts are rewarded in huge proportions. Ironically, most people don't "roll" in life, because . . . they don't know *how* to get there. Well, of course you don't know how to get there, your brain wasn't designed to know the hows or manage logistics. Here's the hook, however, that we see again and again in the game of life:

> Even though you don't know "how,"
> you must nevertheless do something.

All change requires physical action, which has little value for what it may immediately do for you, but awesome strategic worth as it, alone, puts you in reach of Divine Intelligence and her web of potential logistical maneuvers, ordained by your earlier end results.

Which feels weird, at first. I mean, how do you decide on your next step if you don't know how your dream's going to come true? Again, leading many not to take the next step. *But the truth is, it doesn't matter what you do next, so long as you do something to the best of your ability that moves you in the direction that at least makes the most sense, given your options!* You could even go in the opposite direction as your system is telling you to go, which may be "south on Main Street" when you're supposed to go north, yet eventually you're going to hear, over Barry Manilow, "Make a legal U-turn!" This type of guidance, however, is not forthcoming when your car's in park! Do anything, go anywhere, even to a sucky job you hate, if the alternative is sitting at home, waiting for your "ship to come in." As the Universe once pointed out in a note, "The only time the ship of your dreams will never find you is if you are at home, waiting for it." Also relevant, the Universe once said,

---

A Note from the Universe

If you go first and reach for the fruit, I'll shake the tree.

Do a little dance; I'll add some music.

Move in the direction of your dreams, even though at first nothing seems to happen; I'll align the stars, butter your bread, connect the dots, trim the hedge, move some mountains, float the boat, and see you at the ball.

Metaphorically. Except for seeing you at the ball.

If you go first,
The Universe

P.S. Smile, wink, and saunter, and whoa . . .
I'll put some rumble in the jungle.

Understand That the "Miracles" of Progress Are Usually Invisible

There's another interesting parallel in this GPS analogy. For example, at what point in a three-hour guided journey to a new friend's home for afternoon tea, in a town you've never been to before in your life, would you realize the system worked flawlessly? At what point would you realize that every left- and right-hand turn you were told to take were perfect, spot-on miracles? Right! Not until you finally arrived! Not until the final seconds of the entire journey! Meaning, at two hours and 59 minutes into the journey, everything would still look weird! New and unfamiliar, no sign of your friend, right? Leaving you at risk to prejudge, "It isn't working for me. It works for all my friends, but not me. I must have invisible, limiting, self-sabotaging beliefs. I think I'll go back home and watch *The Secret* 30 more times in 30 more days." But all the while, *it was working for you!* You just couldn't see it, *yet.*

Again, this is when faith enters the picture. We do not have the benefit of physically seeing our friend as an ant-like dot on the horizon waving us onward; we see nothing. Yet through understanding "miracles," we realize that this system we're learning to play *always works*! It always works *for you*. You can't even turn it off. Not if you wanted to. And so, no matter what your eyes are showing you, *know it's working*. Let this become your mantra: "I can't see it, but it's working. It always works. It never fails. Every day I get closer. Every day it gets easier. It's working." Understand that everything you say registers with the Universe. "Oh, it's not working, is it?" reveals limiting beliefs, unintended end results, and confusion. Listen. Correct. Rephrase that which doesn't serve you.

Avoid the Bermuda Triangle of Manifesting

As with any set of guidelines or instructions, these steps for living deliberately and creating consciously have a few nuances. Nothing that doesn't have a happy and easy workaround, if you know what to look out for. Yet if you know not of these nuances, "Uh-oh!"

To explain, do you remember the first time you got a glimpse of life's truths? Maybe it was when you first watched *The Secret* or read a certain book? You were probably bouncing off the walls with glee. "I knew it! I knew it! I'm powerful! All things are possible! We're not here to be judged! Dreams really can come true!" You probably annoyed the heck out of your friends, right? Well, if a young friend or relative, a niece or a nephew, had tripped on by during this time in your life, you probably would've sat them down and said, "You listen to me and listen good: Everything's possible! You need to have dreams! Big dreams! Shoot for the stars! Whatever you want, you can have! Anything! The Universe loves you! There's a law of attraction! Your thoughts become things!" And their eyes would've lighted up as they asked, "I can have anything?" "You bet! Anything you want. Name it!" "Anything?" "Yes, *ANYTHING!* Can't you hear me?!" "Okay . . . I know what I want . . . *I want Bobby's green bike!*" Oh . . . crap. Now you're backpedaling because they can't have Bobby's green bike. That's Bobby's. Even though you just told them they could have *anything*. This is a new nuance.

The workaround is easy, happy, awesome! "You can't have Bobby's green bike, but . . . *you can have your own green bike!* And then you and Bobby can ride your green bikes into the sunset. Whoohoo!"

This is a lighthearted example to show how the nuances work. When serious stuff is in play, there's no margin for error. You need to know the nuances. There are three of them, and together they form the Bermuda Triangle of Manifesting:

You enter the Bermuda Triangle of Manifesting when you *insist upon or attach your hopes to the following end results*:

1. Details – Don't waste your time pining for unimportant details (such as whether the bike is Bobby's, or even whether it's green). Moreover, know that all details are unimportant. You can want them, just don't insist upon them.

2. Hows – Surrender and let go of how you think, or how you may want, your dream to come true—these are the "cursed hows."

3. Specific people – Release yourself of any expectations
    you may have for the specific behavior of
    specific people.

Much more will be said about each of these prongs of the
triangle later; for now what's important is realizing they exist.
Disregarding them as you dream new dreams will put you on a
very slippery slope that will ultimately and assuredly lead to some
successful hits, some crushing misses, and a broken heart. Leaving you bewildered and blaming yourself, your parents, your past
lives, or anything that moves. Meanwhile, it was just a tiny misunderstanding, a nuance, that could have easily been averted if you
had used the Matrix to wisely define what it is you most wanted.
Indeed, the main reason for this whole book.

IT GETS BETTER—*WAY*

Sound exciting? Too good to be true? Apart from your life
being the proof of all shared so far, you might be wise to ask,
"What gives here? How could I be so powerful? What's the point?"

Can you not see that this chapter speaks to an inescapable and
profound order found throughout the universe? One that puts you
at the helm of your adventures? That effectively endows you with
seemingly supernatural powers? Doesn't this power explain how
ordinary people have achieved extraordinary results in their life,
created great artistic works, made heroic comeback saves, amassed
incomprehensible wealth, healed from presumably incurable dis-
eases, and much more? Do you not see how those people were not
saints, selfless, or even brilliant? Do you think their accomplish-
ments were random or destined? Or are you beginning to see that
there are methods, ways, and means to living deliberately and creating consciously, available to all?

Suffice to say, whatever your belief, or lack thereof, in a God,
or the Universe, or Source, it doesn't take much to see that something's going on here in the jungles of time and space. Something
wondrous and awesome—and that we are at the center of it all. Let
me again make a proposition that you can take or leave. We are of,

by, and for the very intelligence that set the cosmos into place. We came here as particles of this intelligence. It is much more than who we are, yet we are fully, 100 percent part of it—just as my toes are pure Mike Dooley, they are not all of me. Therefore, however comparatively small we are, we must still be pure "It." If not, then what are we, where would we have come from, what would we be made of? Mustn't everything be made of the same "stuff"? Could there be this intelligence, and then all other stuff? Or mustn't the intelligence be so primal and necessary that it would have had to create all else, from itself? I trust this is making some sense. If not, that's fine. You don't have to agree with this, but you ought to at least come up with your own answers that explain the stunning order we see everywhere that is undeniable, which I believe will start a quest that will bring you full circle back to these same, simple conclusions. I'm not saying exactly what this Divine Intelligence is, just that it is and we are of it.

Following my line of thinking, an explanation for our presence here can be inferred: from the loftiest part of our being, we (or our greater being, this very intelligence itself) had to have chosen to be here (as us). Otherwise, it would be random and outside of the order we see everywhere. Yes? And so, from that lofty place of choice, we had to have known what we were doing, that it would have been for beautiful, loving reasons that will one day make sense, and that in the meantime, given our evidenced power that I will further be teaching you how to harness, we would have only come here to totally blow the lid off our lives in the most wonderful, mind-bending ways. Ergo, despite what our experiences have been so far, we have built-in default settings to thrive in abundance, health, happiness, and in every way imaginable. *Don't our lives evidence as much?*

We're like giant tidal waves of joy, that have no doubt been careening through existence, now temporarily on planet Earth, with a propensity to succeed in whatever we choose to apply ourselves? A propensity, not a destiny, that simply requires an understanding of the mechanics that bring all things to pass. You, dear reader, came here to hit home runs, to fall in love, and to be happy. So great is this propensity, it's as if your positive thoughts, which are therefore in alignment with my little thesis here, are at least 10,000 times more powerful than your negative thoughts, which are so not in alignment with this thesis. Accordingly, it's as if you're being pushed on to greatness every single day, that for you, opportunity never stops knocking, there is always another way to move forward, a new day to enjoy, and more friends that even now await finding and falling in love with you. Don't we see this everywhere? And yes, you may argue we also see a lot of pain—but not nearly to the degree we see love, joy, and success!

You, even, should be known as, if not already, the comeback kid. You have stunning rebounding abilities, smile more than you frown, laugh more than you cry, have health more than you've been sick, have clarity more than you've been confused, have friends more than you've been alone, and have money more than you've been broke. Yes, you, already. Can you even imagine where your life might be going once you habitually see this? Once you fully understand and begin harnessing your power? Get out of your way? Stop micromanaging the unimportant? Once performing miracles becomes commonplace? All of which, in large part, is why you're here in this world; why you've found this book; why Divine Intelligence wanted to be exactly who you now are? Sheez. Can you not sense that perhaps your confusion, like everyone else's, was part of our choice? To be born into ignorance, so that we might ultimately figure out our power and set ourselves free, *"Yee-ha!"*?

UNDERSTANDING "MIRACLES"

Your default settings are to thrive, to live in abundance with grace, style, ease, health, and all that your heart desires. The steps that will get you there are easy. Our part is always the easy part. But if we don't know to do our part, or what it even is, things will seem to get out of hand in a hurry. To recap some of the most important lessons of this chapter:

1. You don't have to know all things to know yourself and how to create change.

2. You are a streaming manifestor. Worry not how you do this, just notice that you do.

3. Your thoughts become things, your words give you wings.

4. Believing the illusions are "real" ignites passion, inspires dreams, and sparks adventure.

5. For these reasons, and many more, you are inclined to succeed.

TRY THIS AT HOME

What's the main reason you'd like to learn how to live deliberately and create consciously? What might you say is the one thing most on your mind as the main thing you'd like to bring, change, or manifest into your life, and why?

Most on my mind for transformation:

_____

Why this is important to me:

1. _____

2. _____

3. _____

In the next chapter, we'll be learning about ideal end results and your related motivation for wanting them, after which you'll be asked to revisit this list to see how your values stack up. Then, in Chapter 3, we'll do a new version of this little exercise.

Chapter 2

THE MATRIX

A Note from the Universe

Ever notice how when someone dreams of happiness, abundance, health, romance, or friendship, they never have to wonder if it's in their best interest?

But when someone dreams of a specific house, employer, love interest, deadline, dollar amount, or diet fad, they often end up contradicting themselves?

Keep your "end results" general. Everything else is just a "how."

To the big picture,
The Universe

P.S. By the way, I dream of your happiness.

It's peculiar how when we first learn of our power, how much we're loved, and how free we've always been, the first thing we try to do is micromanage our lives—putting ourselves in the right place, at the right time, with the right people, managing our p's and q's, thinking that if we look after the pennies, the pounds will look after themselves, as my British mum used to say. Actually, Mum, there's a much better way to manifest pounds.

This micromanagement puts the cart before the horse and the weight of the world on our shoulders, as we let the cursed hows drag us straight to the center of the Bermuda Triangle of

Manifesting. We think once we can manage the details, the hows, and the people in our lives, boy oh boy will we be happy. Doesn't work like that.

Twelve years ago, on the hoped-for verge of my second World Tour, as I was struggling to find a new angle for sharing that our "thoughts become things," I wrote down on a piece of paper various *types* of end results. Drawing arrows, labeling columns, and writing descriptors, I suddenly realized that in front of my eyes a loose and rough table, a Matrix, was forming. Today, it's this very Matrix, now refined, that I continue to share with others as a way to clearly identify what we really want, in a way that frees up life's magic to bring it to us in the shortest, quickest, most harmonious way. This Matrix, then, is the starting point of a program that gives us direction for ramping up excitement and taking action, toward living the life of our dreams.

Consider our GPS navigation analogy. If there are only two steps you must take to trigger a manifestation, 1) Know your end result and 2) Take action, then getting each right is rather important—to an enormous degree. And while there are books and teachings galore extolling the virtue of "taking massive, or inspired, action," there are none that I know of extolling the virtue of wisely choosing your end results, in form and with rationale. The Matrix is 100 percent about this Step 1. At its heart lies a simple yet *highly unexpected* concept for creating personal transformation. *Playing* the Matrix then pulls both steps together.

What this chapter reveals is that for the most assured successes—nearing 100 percent dependability, save for mass global events and trends that no one can manipulate[1]—you must have a *big picture* approach to creating change, foregoing the often *encouraged* micromanagement approach, thereby:

1. Achieving clarity in purpose and desire to avoid contradictions and self-sabotage

2. Fueling your dreams with passion while not attaching to unimportant details

---

1   More on this later in the chapter, under Global Events and Trends.

3. Planning and acting on your dreams without
    "messing with the cursed hows"!

HOW WE GOT IT SO WRONG

Choosing as we did to be born into spiritually primitive times like these, early in the evolutionary scale of consciousness, we knew that great ignorance would roam the lands. A consequence of our relatively immediate ancestral naiveties, having just crawled out of the caves, is that to this day we give great priority to our physical senses over our inner senses. Most people don't even know they have inner senses; they're certainly not taught in school alongside smelling, hearing, and tasting. And so, when it comes to deciding what to do with our lives and the courses we'll chart, virtually no one is told to feel their way, use their instincts, trust and have faith; instead we're admonished to get logical. "You better figure it out, young lady or young man, because no one's going to figure it out for you!"

So off we trip, using our physical senses alone, not only to rate or judge ourselves, but our paths, and the rest of the world—yikes! We learn to get practical and realistic! We're taught to use our heads, not our hearts. We're involuntarily pushed into becoming micromanagers while training ourselves to tune *out* our leanings, urges, instincts, hunches, and deeper inner knowing.

My Turn

I was no different. Thought I would start small using visualizations and manifestations to aid in my micromanagement of all things, before moving on to global domination. Sometimes it worked, sometimes it didn't, and sometimes it did, but I wished it hadn't. One step forward, one step back. Three steps forward, three steps back. Backfire, ricochet, fall down.

✓ I went out into the world upon graduation and got
the fire-engine-red convertible dream car.

✓ *I crashed my fire-engine-red convertible dream car.*

✓ I landed a coveted job at the then Price Waterhouse.

   ✓ *I discovered, as did the firm, I was the worst auditor they ever hired.*

✓ Saved my job with a transfer into the tax department.

   ✓ *Girlfriend cheated on me.*

✓ Dreamed of a foreign assignment to London, Amsterdam, or Tokyo.

   ✓ *Was relocated to Riyadh, Saudi Arabia.*

✓ Upon repatriation to the USA, I landed my first choice of cities to work in: Boston.

   ✓ *Realized I was not happy as an accountant.*

✓ Was nevertheless promoted to manager at Price Waterhouse.

   ✓ *Sold my home and quit my job.*

✓ Moved to Florida to join some power start-up or otherwise rock the world.

   ✓ *Hopelessly lost, I go into business selling T-shirts from a sidewalk to tourists.*

As micromanagers, we have hits, we have misses, and we have, *"Oh crap, why did I ever want that?!"* Such is the lot of the novice, who finds success so unreliable, so fleeting and sporadic, they draw the false conclusion that either something is wrong with *them* or there must be some other factor involved in determining which thoughts of theirs will become the things and events of their lives. Maybe it's God, the Universe, karma, ancient spiritual contracts, or the like. Whatever they conclude, *they're effectively throwing their power out the window.*

> It's time to let the details take care of themselves while you create space *for even better than you knew to ask for.*

Two Reasons for Our Hits and Misses

Why do we have these hit-or-miss successes when we micromanage? Why does it work one day, not the next, and then, on the third day it works, but we wish it hadn't? Why are our successes anything but assured? Or, why do we sometimes succeed, but at the expense of other dreams? Two reasons, and incidentally, neither one of them are our invisible, limiting, self-sabotaging beliefs. I believe too much time is spent looking for what's invisible, to the degree that some searches end up creating such beliefs. Limited beliefs are relatively easy to crush without even knowing what they are, as you'll find from four Limited-Belief-Busting Freebie Tips I'll offer you later in this book.

The main two reasons, however, that we slip and slide as budding deliberate creators are because of our misunderstandings and contradictions, which of course lead to poorly chosen, or waffling, end results, that often place us in the "Bermuda Triangle." More specifically:

1. Misunderstandings

   a. Our power and responsibilities

   b. The flow of all manifestations

2. Contradictions – The Nuances

    a. Not knowing what we really want

    b. Attaching to the details

    c. Messing with the "cursed hows"

Misunderstanding our power and responsibilities; who we really are, the power of our focus, and what we're truly capable of in time and space. That *living* our lives is up to us. That we already have all we could ever need to get all we could ever want. All covered in Chapter 1. In this chapter, we're about to learn that there's a very real flow to all manifestations. And as the book progresses, we'll review how we (used to) unknowingly contradict ourselves over what we really want. We'll see how attaching to unimportant details may clash with our big-picture priorities and how an insistence upon success reaching us through one door, that in fact may never open, shuts all other doors.

When end results are poorly chosen, bedlam looms. For example, "Great! You've manifested one million dollars in just 12 months!" Yet doing so put you two million in debt. "Super! Trixie took the bait and has fallen head over heels in love with you. She's even moved in and brought her mom!" But then you fall sick. Lose your job. So she leaves you . . . for *Babette*. Or, you've got the Ferrari . . . but to afford it, you live in a tent. Such is the booby-trapped life of a micromanager, which never quite proceeds as expected. Nothing is what you hoped it would be.

THE BIG-PICTURE APPROACH TO PERSONAL TRANSFORMATION

Happily, there's a better way. It will free you from the type of happiness that depends upon specific people, cursed hows, and unimportant details. It's called the Matrix. It's time to let the details take care of themselves while you create space *for even better than you knew to ask for.*

Look at Figure 2.1 and let's go through the Matrix row by row, column by column. (You can see it in color on the back cover of this book.)

The Matrix

← The Entire Spectrum of Reality, Containing All Possible Desires/End Results →

	Thought & Emotion	The Illusions: Dependent on Time, Space, Matter, or Others			
* Ethereal * Highest & Best End Results		Physical: Generalized. Excellent!	Physical: Type 1 Narrower yet reasonable. Begins limiting options.	Physical: Type 2 Significantly dependent on others or aligned beliefs.	Physical: Type 3 Entirely dependent upon others. Worst case cursed hows.
Dependent Solely Upon You		Dependent on the Illusions		Increasingly dependent upon the Illusions and on Others	Entirely dependent on Others
Happiness	Understanding Gratitude Spirituality Confidence Creativity Acceptance Tolerance Compassion Patience Self-Love Etc.	**The Fantastic Five** Livelihood Abundance Health Relationships Appearance Etc.	Possessions Career/Work Wealth Levels Friends Associates Family Harmony Fun & Games $ Amounts Hobbies Fitness Talents Etc.	Projects Events Diet Investments Timelines Type of Car $ Amounts Etc.	Specific… • People • Employer • Customer • Client • Plans • Stock • House • Etc.

← Attach! Attach! Attach! →

← Detach! Detach! Detach! →

← Circumstances (The Universe Manages) →

← Cursed Hows (All on you!) →

Figure 2.1

The Matrix exists entirely as a tool to help you define what it is you most want, *in terms of end results,* in the most effective way possible to bring about rapid transformation. At its core lie six columns, all the rest, above and below these six columns, are simply descriptors:

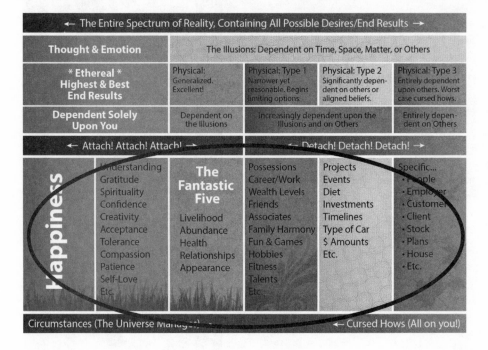

Figure 2.2

The top row tells us that those six columns contain the entire spectrum of reality, all possible desires, dreams, and/or end results. Whatever you have ever wanted, now want, or will want lies in one of these columns:

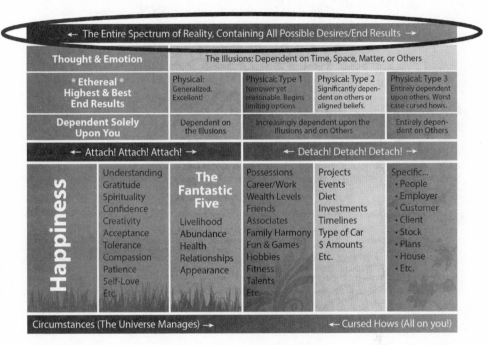

Figure 2.3

On the left side of the Matrix, the first two columns include end results that are defined by your thoughts and your emotions.

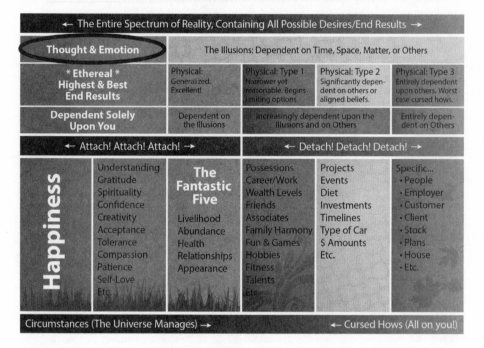

Figure 2.4

Whereas, the next four columns include end results defined by and dependent upon the illusions—all "things" time, space, matter, or other people's thoughts.

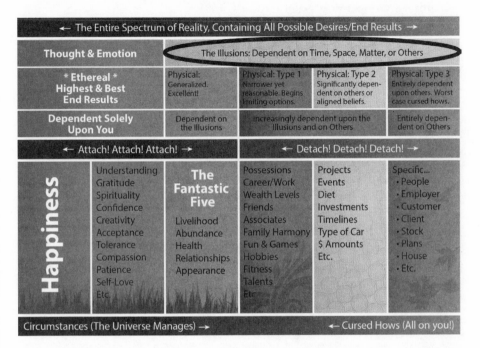

Figure 2.5

Back on the left side of the Matrix, skipping the fourth-row labels that will be self-evident as you understand each of the columns, successful manifestations of the first two end result columns are dependent solely upon you.

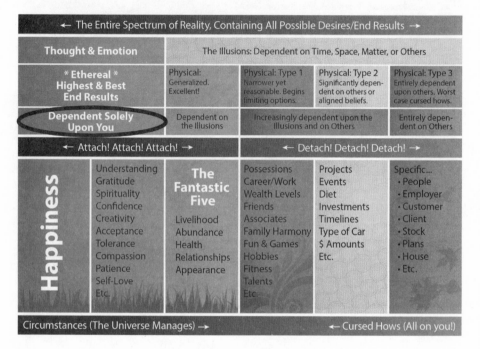

Figure 2.6

Whereas, moving across the Matrix, successful manifestations in the third, fourth, and fifth columns become *increasingly* dependent upon the illusions and/or other people.

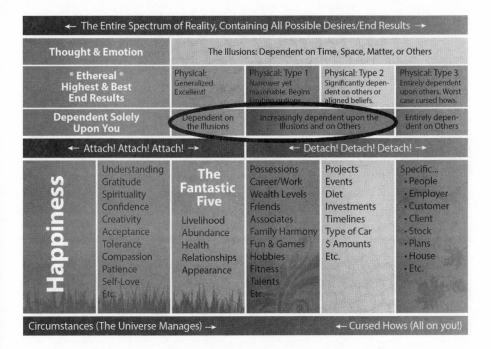

Figure 2.7

And in the red column on the far right, successful manifestations depend, in part, upon someone else, their decisions, and their thoughts.

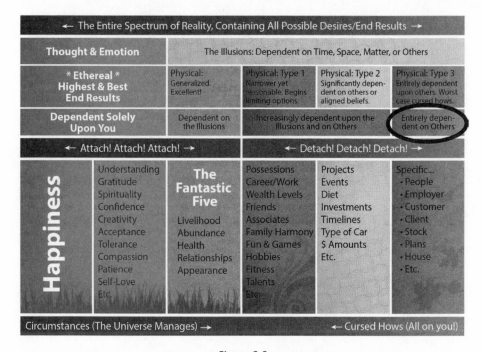

Figure 2.8

Now let's look at each of the main six columns, which offer the deliberate creator a complete palette of any and every imaginable desired end result one may ever dream of doing, being, or having.

Column 1, Happiness

We've heard it all our lives, and we see it portrayed as such here, your happiness is dependent upon your chosen thoughts and emotions, "Happiness is an inside job." Better still, you get to define happiness yourself. I rather dislike when an audience member asks me to define happiness. First, it can and does mean so many different things. Second, the question implies there's probably one answer that is "better" than all others, to which I disagree.

For purposes of Playing the Matrix, you get to define it; play the Matrix well, and you'll get more of whatever your definition was.

Column 2, Understanding, et al.

This column exists to illustrate that there are other ethereal end results, dreams we may choose, dependent solely upon our thoughts and emotions, other than happiness. These are usually not very popular or common dreams, but they're certainly worthy of our consideration: understanding (enlightenment), gratitude, spirituality, confidence, creativity, acceptance, tolerance, compassion, patience, self-love, etc.

Column 3, The Fantastic Five

This is the first column that falls under the heading The Illusions (from the second row). Successful manifestations here depend upon either time, space, matter, or others. Yet contrary to popular thinking, the moniker chosen to label the "five things" is Fantastic, and, as you may have guessed, the color coding (which can be seen on the back cover of this book) has meaning. Like the columns to its left, it's green, as in "Go!"

Two critical points are being deliberately implied by this moniker and color coding, *the rationale for which will follow shortly.*

1. There's nothing unspiritual about the material world, nor wanting to manipulate yours. That some of your dreams may be dependent on the illusions is not a problem. You are, in part, a *physical* being, yourself. And if you want to fill your life with pretty things, fancy cars, or whatever else tangible, go for it—the Matrix will soon show you how.

2. Each of the Fantastic Five components is a generality. Which means, for reasons you shall soon see, the most awesome end results, the easiest to attain with ensured success, are those that are *generally stated*! This is the main operant of the Matrix. So unexpected, right? Hang in there: By the end of the

chapter, this *will* make sense. Keep reading before you go back and reread.

Let's go through each of the Fantastic Five to leave no doubt in your mind as to what they stand for.

1. **Livelihood.** This is why you get out of bed each morning. It has nothing to do with income or money. It could be called your dance with life, mental and physical. You could be dusting the house. You could be tending the garden. You could be watching Oprah. Or you could be a titan on Wall Street. It's what you do every day.

2. **Abundance.** "Abundance" could mean "a great many" of any named thing, emotion, or characteristic, but here, honey, it means money.

3. **Health.** This is your physical body.

4. **Relationships.** This is . . . someone else's physical body.

5. **Appearance.** This is being pleased with your body's aesthetics, not performance or health. It has its own category because we're often obsessed with how much we weigh or don't weigh, as well as otherwise altering our looks. If that's a priority for you, go for it! You're worthy. You deserve to be happy in any area you choose to focus.

Column 4, Physical: Type 1

We're getting narrower with our descriptions. We're beginning to refine and thereby limit our scope by getting more specific than any of the first three columns. This column is made up of details that would otherwise automatically be included in the Fantastic Five.

Column 5, Physical: Type 2

Now our dreams and end results are getting even more detailed, and their manifestations are therefore becoming increasingly dependent on invisible and unknown considerations, other people, and/or our own aligned beliefs.

Column 6, Physical: Type 3

Successful manifestations of these end results are dependent upon other people and their thoughts (as much as our own); these are worst-case examples of "cursed hows." Hoping and wanting specific people to behave in specific ways, thinking that this is how *we'll* ultimately find happiness.

That's the gamut of where your end results can be, all six columns, from left to right; from the ethereal to the material to other people.

Game On

Now let's talk strategy. I've already hinted that the green columns are choicest, but as for rationale, in which columns do you think we should ideally focus our attention and energy for maximum returns as we begin to play the Matrix?

Firstly, on which side of the Matrix did we say success was dependent solely on you? The left. And on which side did we say it was partly dependent on others? The right.

Wouldn't it then make sense to start out on the left side, in the left-most columns, where we're in control, as opposed to starting out with columns on the right, where others are also in control? Right.

Secondly, even cooler and far more compelling, remember the Big Bang mention in the previous chapter? Where did we say all manifestations start—yours, mine, and the Divine's? Thought. Thought of *end results*. And we said, the end in mind forces the details. Thought forces circumstance, as well as inspiration, courage, *and all else needed for you to get all you want*. So, what's the "thought" side of the Matrix? The left. What's the "thing" side? The right. And there you have it, thoughts become things, *the flow beneath all manifestations and across the Matrix.*

The Entire Spectrum of Reality, Containing All Possible Desires/End Results →				
Thought & Emotion	The Illusions: Dependent on Time, Space, Matter, or Others			
* Ethereal * **Highest & Best End Results**	Physical: Generalized. Excellent!	Physical: Type 1 Narrower yet reasonable. Begins limiting options.	Physical: Type 2 Significantly dependent on others or aligned beliefs.	Physical: Type 3 Entirely dependent upon others. Worst case cursed hows.
Dependent Solely Upon You	Dependent on the Illusions	Increasingly dependent upon the Illusions and on Others		Entirely dependent on Others
← Attach! Attach! Attach! →		← Detach! Detach! Detach! →		
Happiness	Understanding Gratitude Spirituality Confidence Creativity Acceptance Tolerance Compassion Patience Self-Love Etc.	**The Fantastic Five** Livelihood Abundance Health Relationships Appearance	Possessions Career/Work Wealth Levels Friends Associates Family Harmony Fun & Games Hobbies Fitness Talents Etc.	Projects Events Diet Investments Timelines Type of Car $ Amounts Etc.	Specific... • People • Employer • Customer • Client • Stock • Plans • House • Etc.
◄ Circumstances (The Universe Manages) →			← Cursed Hows (All on you!)	

Figure 2.9

Notice the bottom row, circled: it says, "Circumstances (The Universe Manages)." When we play the Matrix with end results on the left side, Divine Intelligence arranges all we need to have all we want, emotionally and physically, *including all the details to the right of the column we start in.*

Of course, again, we still have to physically show up, car in gear, take action, but this is not the action chapter. It's the "choose your end results wisely" chapter.

A Note from the Universe

Reality is not what your eyes show your mind, but what your mind creates for your eyes to see. You're not limited by logic, the past, or the world around you. You're not even of the world around you. You're supernatural, pure spirit.

Magic, miracles, and luck are the consequences of understanding this, the inevitable result of dreaming and acting in spite of appearances. Most essentially, if you can imagine an end result, and move with it, you can have it.

You are ever so close,
The Universe

THE OLD WAY OF BLOOD, SWEAT, AND TEARS

From which side of the Matrix do most people have their end results when they want to create change in their life, the left or the right?

The right. And most often, they start out in the red column! Rationalizing, "My life will *finally* take off once you show me respect at home, once I get a raise at work, and when the kids start making their beds before school every day." In their mind, by beginning on the right side of the Matrix, they reason if the details can be micromanaged, they will then have a happier family, leading to a fuller life, leading to more confidence and creativity, leading to self-love, finally leading to happiness for all involved, and they expect to march across the Matrix from right to left! In other words, once everyone else behaves as they want them to, their life will soar.

This is a classic case of messing with the cursed hows, indicated by the bottom row of the Matrix, "Cursed Hows (All on you)!" now circled in Figure 2.10.

One of two huge fails arises when you start Playing the Matrix on the right:

1. *It might not work, ever.* Larry King, legendary talk show host on CNN, asked one of his two panels on *The Secret* if "this law of attraction works for everything?" And on the spot, caught off guard in front of millions of viewers, the answer was a timid, "Yeah, Larry. I don't see why not?" But with a little thought and not having to answer this under the pressure of live TV, let me tell you, *"No way, José!* The law of attraction absolutely does not work on all things!"

    a. You can't manipulate other people. They too have dominion over their circumstances.

    b. You can't insist on *how* your dream will come true when there are seven billion co-creators, unexpected trends, unpredictable markets, economies, politics, and many more co-creations heaving and ho-ing.

    c. Nor can you demand unimportant details manifest without risking:

        i. success at the expense of other, invisibly linked details, including those that were even better than you knew to hope for, and/or

        ii. failure because such details were tied to specific people or hows.

2. *It might work, but not make you happy.* Even when you sometimes succeed with micromanagement (because, as your life has shown you, sometimes it works!), there's no flow from right to left. Things *do not* become thoughts. Right? And thus, there's no assurance (and little chance) of those successes alone making you happy.

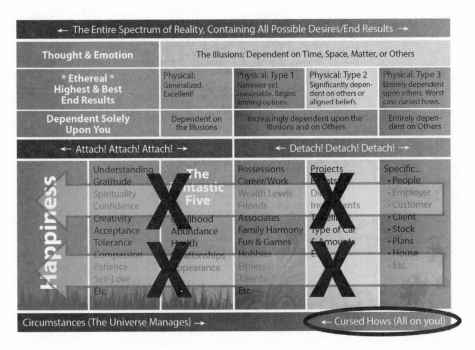

Figure 2.10

THE ULTIMATE END RESULT

Based on how I placed the lettering in the six columns, can you guess the ultimate end result?

Happiness!? Right, which even jibes with old-school teachings, except our Matrix-based answer is for totally different reasons.

First, we've often been taught that happiness is what really matters, *because material things don't*. Why can't they both matter? Why can't happiness be a state of mind *and* a vehicle toward greater abundance, health, harmony, and all else your heart desires?

Occasionally a timid hand would be raised during earlier presentations of this Matrix, "Mike, I get what you're saying, that happiness is the ultimate end result, but . . . well, what if that's all I get? Just . . . happy?"

This question came up frequently, from various audiences, before I saw its merit. The real question they were all asking was, "What if I get really, genuinely happy, but I'm still broke, unemployed, confused, live in a tent, and become so sick I have open, oozing sores on my face? Happiness isn't going to pay my bills, is it?" *As if* the Universe needs to be told, "Happy . . . *and* healthy, working, playing, surrounded by friends, and enough money to live life on my own terms." Do you think if you remembered to tell the Universe you wanted to be healthy, you'd have to also add, "Not just healthy, but with all of my digits, possessing excellent hearing and vision, with no need for medication, and able to keep up with my friends"? If we had to name every conceivable detail truly required for us to be healthy, or happy, the list could be many miles long and would still remain grossly incomplete! *You don't have to name the details that are otherwise required for the manifestation of what you dream of, to imply their inclusion in the life of your dreams.* The same is true for any qualities or dispensations that happiness requires. They will be arranged for you, including money, as long as you named, insisted upon, and physically moved toward being happier, in every area of your life, including financially.

> We've been told health is our natural state. But we haven't been told being a millionaire is our natural state. Just the opposite, and so we've manifested just the opposite.

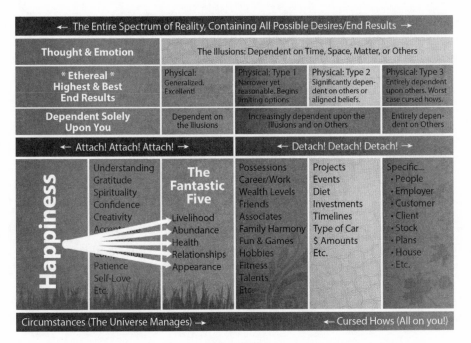

The Entire Spectrum of Reality, Containing All Possible Desires/End Results →				
Thought & Emotion	The Illusions: Dependent on Time, Space, Matter, or Others			
* Ethereal * Highest & Best End Results	Physical: Generalized. Excellent!	Physical: Type 1 Narrower yet reasonable. Begins limiting options.	Physical: Type 2 Significantly dependent on others or aligned beliefs.	Physical: Type 3 Entirely dependent upon others. Worst case cursed hows.
Dependent Solely Upon You	Dependent on the Illusions	Increasingly dependent upon the Illusions and on Others		Entirely dependent on Others
← Attach! Attach! Attach! →		← Detach! Detach! Detach! →		
Happiness	Understanding Gratitude Spirituality Confidence Creativity Accep... ... Patience Self-Love Etc.	**The Fantastic Five** Livelihood Abundance Health Relationships Appearance	Possessions Career/Work Wealth Levels Friends Associates Family Harmony Fun & Games Hobbies Fitness Talents Etc.	Projects Events Diet Investments Timelines Type of Car $ Amounts Etc.	Specific... • People • Employer • Customer • Client • Stock • Plans • House • Etc.
Circumstances (The Universe Manages) →		← Cursed Hows (All on you!)		

Figure 2.11

Second, to be clear. The kind of happiness implied in the leftmost column of the Matrix is not the *I-can-learn-to-love-this-as-I-lower-my-expectations-and-settle-for-what-I-have* kind of happiness. It's the *Whoohoo!-I-love-my-life!-Hot-dang-shut-the-door-get-out-of-town-life-rocks-and-so-do-I!* kind of happiness. And the only way you're going be *that* happy is if "all the cylinders" of the major categories in your life are firing. The only way such happiness can authentically be experienced (made manifest; thoughts become things) in the dreamer's life, is if pretty much everything in their life starts working, tangible and intangible, material and ethereal. Huge happiness as an end result or dream *implies* the reason for it will be your whole life taking off, as you're fulfilled, busy yet rested, surrounded by friends, laughter, and love! Not because you're delusional or easily satisfied. Which isn't to say we can't find happiness, today, in our lives, pre-transformation. In fact, this is also part of the Matrix equation, as you will soon see.

With happiness as your end result, you don't even have to think of money, or any of the Fantastic Five categories, to attract them into your life. Just as, for many of us, we don't even have to think about health to have health. We've been told health is our natural state. But we haven't been told being a millionaire is our natural state. Just the opposite, and so we've manifested just the opposite. Yet for having wisely chosen end results, followed by taking action, we can ultimately erase any old beliefs that may have once denied us, even if we haven't yet identified all those old beliefs! This concept will be elaborated on shortly.

Happiness is the ultimate end result, because it's the only end result that implies all the major cylinders are firing in the Fantastic Five column, *just as those cylinders are then implying that all the details to their right are also lining up in ways that would thrill you*, orchestrated and arranged by Divine Mind, just as they were upon the Big Bang for the creation of the physical cosmos.

NUANCES WITHIN THE NUANCES

You can, of course, start out with end results *in any column you choose*. If you're on the right side, you may not succeed, but you're free to try. Any deviation from Happiness as your starting point has implications that need to be understood. There are even nuances within the nuances. Let me explain another significant operant of the Matrix that we just brushed into to make it as plain as day:

Everything to the right of your starting point, to the right of the column you begin within, necessary to manifest your desired starting point, will be arranged meticulously for you as you show up and take action in your dream's direction. All that's to the right of your starting point *not* necessary for its manifestation will be unaffected.

Well, everything is to the right of happiness, and as we just laid out, it's all necessary to be *rocking, whoohoo happy*! But let's just say, *for illustrative purposes only*, that all you care about is money,

money, money, perhaps because you mistakenly think that with lots of it, all else in your life will automatically come together.

Show Me the Money

This is only for illustration purposes; hopefully it's not remotely true for you. Not that there's anything unspiritual about money, but if it's *all* you think about, let me show you how things may shake out in your life.

If you keep your desire for money general, you'll be starting out in the third column, the Fantastic Five; and if you get emotionally excited about it as I'll teach in Chapter 4, and you take action on it, as I'll teach in Chapter 5, *it has to happen, you will be financially rich!* It's actually not difficult to do; just look at the people in the world who have financial abundance . . . Not necessarily the sharpest tools in the shed, are they? Whoohoo! Which means neither do we have to be! We just have to know which buttons to press and which levers to pull. They did it accidentally; we can do it deliberately. But in this example, if money is all you care about, as you physically do what you can to move toward it, everything to the right of your starting point *necessary* to manifest it will be arranged, but nothing else.

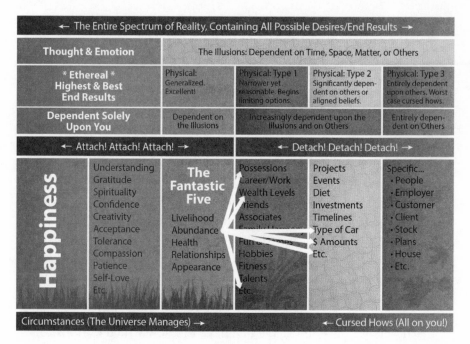

← The Entire Spectrum of Reality, Containing All Possible Desires/End Results →			
Thought & Emotion	The Illusions: Dependent on Time, Space, Matter, or Others		
* Ethereal * **Highest & Best** **End Results**	Physical: Generalized. Excellent!	Physical: Type 1 Narrower yet reasonable. Begins limiting options.	Physical: Type 2 Significantly depen- dent on others or aligned beliefs.	Physical: Type 3 Entirely dependent upon others. Worst case cursed hows.
Dependent Solely **Upon You**	Dependent on the Illusions	Increasingly dependent upon the Illusions and on Others		Entirely depen- dent on Others
← Attach! Attach! Attach! →		← Detach! Detach! Detach! →	

Figure 2.12

The arrows above reflect Abundance as your chosen starting point for creating transformation, and they extend to the elements in the blue and yellow columns that will *automatically* be arranged for you as you continue to live your life, moving in its direction.

So, once you've manifested $20 million, for example, this is how your life will shake out:

Manifested	**Not Affected**
Possessions	Career/Work
Wealth Levels	Friends
Type of Car	Associates
$ Amounts	Family Harmony
Other stuff (Etc.)	Fun & Games
	Hobbies
	Fitness
	Talents
	Projects
	Events
	Diet
	Investments
	Timelines
	Other stuff (Etc.)

Further, there's *nothing* assured in the red column, because such manifestations will depend significantly upon specific people and their thoughts. As for the columns above, you might wonder whether Career/Work would be transformed to your liking, since money often stems from both. But the hows are not our domain. You want abundance, the Universe knows the shortest, quickest way, given the maze of all else you think and want. What if abundance were to reach you through an inheritance? The lottery? A lawsuit? Do you see how it's quite conceivable that you will manifest abundance, but in less than desirable ways?

Two things are most striking:

1. Most of your life will not change simply because you have a lot of money, and,

2. While you *will* manifest abundance, it's in the third column! And as you saw, there's no flow from right to left, *from Abundance to Happiness*. You'll get your money, but little else, and for this, you will be quite the unhappy camper—as is always the case for the person who *only* cares about money.

Where Art Thou, Romeo?

This time, let's say, *for illustrative purposes only*, all you care about is finding your Romeo or Juliet. That's it. You care about nothing else, maybe because you mistakenly think that with "true love" (as in, a dreamy partner), all else in your life will take care of itself. Now, finding a romantic partner is well within the Fantastic Five, excellent. If you do all else outlined in this book, mostly creating excitement and showing up, you are guaranteed to find him or her. There're seven and a half billion candidates out there and Divine Mind can hook you up *right*. But in this scenario, now that you've found them, if they in fact were all you cared about, how will the rest of your life shake out?

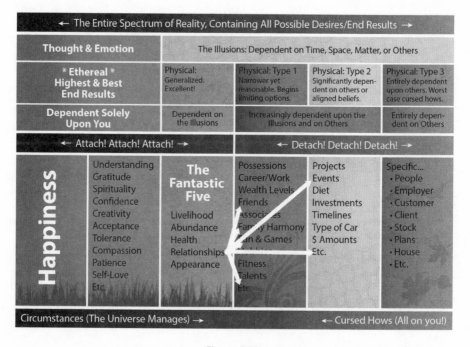

Figure 2.13

The arrows in Figure 2.13 reflect Relationships (in this case, romantic) as your chosen starting point for creating transformation, and they extend to the elements in the blue and yellow columns that will *automatically* be arranged for you as you continue to live your life, moving in its direction.

So, once you've found your honey, for example, this is how your life will likely shake out:

Manifested	Not Affected
Friends	Possessions
Family Harmony	Career/Work
Fun & Games	Wealth Levels
Events	Associates
Other stuff (Etc.)	Hobbies
	Fitness
	Talents
	Projects
	Diets
	Investments
	Timelines
	Type of Car
	$ Amounts
	Other stuff (Etc.)

Again, there's *nothing* assured in the red column, because such manifestations will depend significantly upon *specific* people and their thoughts. As for the columns above, I was exceedingly generous, assuming that with your newfound love, those named areas of your life in the first column would similarly bloom.

Still, two things are striking:

1. Most of your life will *not* change simply because you've "found love," and,

2. While you *will* manifest your Romeo, your starting point was in the third column of the Matrix, and there's no flow from right to left, *from Romeo to*

Happiness. You'll have a partner, but little else is assured. You may both be without fulfilling livelihoods, broke, living in a leaking tent, and finding that the open, oozing sores on your face were contagious! How *happy* will you two lovebirds be?

Of course, in either of these two illustrative examples, you needn't have been so single-minded. As we will soon review, you can have multiple priorities and end results at the same time, including Happiness, which alone implies all the cylinders are firing. More on diversifying in just a bit.

BUT . . . BUT . . . BUT!

Is this starting to make sense? I'd imagine you're mostly on board, but not all the way. If I were to end my explanation now, I'm pretty sure within 24 hours you'd have objections. Major objections. You'd feel both confused and betrayed. "The audacity! This can't be right. This completely contradicts so many other theories and teachings on the law of attraction that advocate getting into all the luscious details!"

So, allow me to head you off at the pass. Let me bring to your attention and put into words those objections and seeming contradictions that would soon be flooding your mind and show you all is well, and that in fact there are *zero contradictions.*

"Never attach to the outcome."

You've probably read in great book after great book or heard from great speaker after great speaker, "*Never attach to the outcome.* That's your problem, you're attaching your hopes, expectations, and happiness to outcomes." Right? And aren't *outcome* and *end result* synonymous? And doesn't it seem like I'm saying, "Every manifestation begins with your desired outcome, and so you must attach to it!" And yes, indeed, that is *exactly* what I've been saying. Wow, how do we reconcile this?

Easy. No contradiction whatsoever. Where in the Matrix are most people's desired outcomes, those things or circumstances they want to manifest? On the left or right side? They're on the right! Thin ice! Slippery slope! *If that is where your dreams now lie*, detach!!

But you know better. We've reviewed the Matrix, you're getting this. So, where in the Matrix will your desired outcomes now be? If you've followed along in this chapter and have a new sense of what's really important to you, you'd choose to be on the left. This means you now have entirely different kinds of end results, more focused on happiness and big-picture values, which will warrant an entirely different approach to bringing them about. Now there are new rules. The Matrix creates a new paradigm. Now there are new guidelines. To orchestrate change and transformation beginning with the Matrix means beginning with a *generally stated end in mind* and attaching to it, settling for nothing less than what it is you most want. Holding out your proverbial cup until it's overflowing. Insist. Demand. No contradiction.

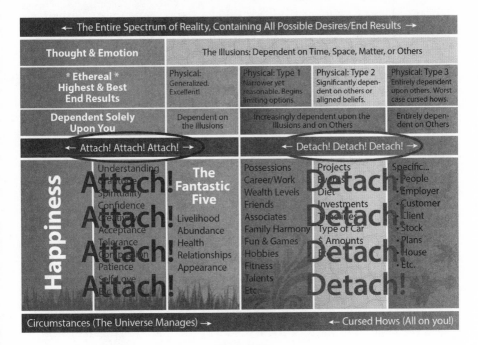

Figure 2.14

"But, Mike, what about vision boards?"

Vision boards, scrapbooks, pictures on the refrigerator, and similar visual tools are used to spark the process of envisioning. Even I taught vision boards and scrapbooks in *Infinite Possibilities*. Yet with such images all being of people and things that would reside on the right side of the Matrix, suddenly it seems these props may be problematic. Not really.

As you likely realize, sometimes words slip when applied to truth, and so we need to look beneath them for the intention they were meant to carry by the person choosing them. This kind of slippage can also happen with pictures on vision boards. It depends on what those images or pictures mean to you to determine whether you're playing the Matrix backward.

For example, two people could theoretically have the exact same vision board. For one person, the images represent absolutes: "That's my new car. And that circle of friends laughing at my jokes on spring break last summer in Cancun, they'll always love me and laugh at my jokes. And that house on the hill? That's my next house. Even though it's not for sale . . . and someone now lives there, it's mine. *This* job with *that* company, they're going to give me a corner office! *This* title or *that* label in ABC industry, that's who I really am." Interpreted like this, those pictures clearly reflect an attachment and insistence upon details, circumstances, and specific people's approval, all coming from the right side of the Matrix. Not cool.

But take the other person who has the same vision board: "That's the *type* of car I want next. See that house and its modern kitchen? *Just like* where I'll soon be living! And these are the *kinds of* friends and awesome vacations that I'll take every year, surrounded by love and laughter. You know, I'd like to work in this profession, probably in this career, but I'm open to something even better." Now those same images are not being seen as end results, but as by-products of an exciting, expanding, tailor-crafted life. A "rocking life" is this person's end result, which is on the left side of the Matrix. Their images are just the frosting on the cake, but it's the cake that matters, the left side of the Matrix. They're using the detailed photos of things from the right side of the Matrix to get excited about how amazing their life is going to be on the left side. They're leaving room for surprises, which is what this Matrix creates space for.

So, details are fine, but *not as end results!* They're awesome to get you excited about your big-picture dreams that are otherwise general and vague. The scrapbook or vision board is getting you excited about the kind of feelings and the rocking life you're going to be having. The images are reflective of the *type and kinds* of things or friends that will be in your life. Used like this, a vision board is "rocket fuel" for greater clarity, more excitement, and therefore faster manifestations, whereas seen incorrectly, the same vision board becomes a ball and chain *preventing* transformation. More on this notion of using details to create excitement lies in Chapter 4, which is all about how to get into the minutiae without losing site of what you really want.

If your vision board is all about manifesting the exact things pictured, it's problematic. If it's about getting you excited about wonderful changes coming on the left side of the Matrix, that will then spin these or better details, it's very powerful.

A Note from the Universe

In a slightly different world, if dogs believed in "soul mates" when it came to choosing their owners, can you imagine how lonesome most would be?

"Cute Dachshund ISO cool human with nice house near beach. Must be mind-reader, watch Animal Planet, and listen to Dr. Dre. No pic, no reply."

Oh, there's definitely room for "picky," but let there also be room for "surprise me."

Surprise me,
The Universe

"Be careful of what you wish for because you just might get it."

You've heard this forever, right? What a bummer! Why should we have to be careful of what we wish for, particularly given our superpowers and that we're alive in a paradise of illusions where we're inclined to succeed? This admonition implies the world's stage is booby-trapped, that we can't trust ourselves to know what's best for us, or that we ought not want anything, just learn to roll with what comes.

With what we just learned, however, let's again consider where most people's wishes land, in terms of the six columns in the Matrix—the right side. And of course, we now know this means they might have a hit, a miss, or a regret! Yikes! Right, they can't even be careful enough when their dreams start out on the right side of the Matrix. It's just a matter of time, and they're going down.

Consider, however, our new approach of beginning on the left side of the Matrix. Do you think they have to be careful of what they wish for, if it's happiness, fulfillment, friendships, laughter, and enough money to live their life on their terms? "Oh dear, do excuse me, I beg your forgiveness. My doctor warned me but I didn't listen; you see, I've been just too happy lately."

That old saying no longer applies *to our new approach.*

"There are more tears shed over answered prayers than over unanswered prayers."

This sentiment, attributed to mystic philosopher and Roman Catholic Saint Teresa of Ávila and popular in the Bible Belt of the USA, now makes perfect sense, because with just a little contemplation, we realize that even the prayerfully pious *are micromanagers!* Their prayers invariably land on the right side of the Matrix. "Dear God, please let Billy Bob do *this*, and Auntie May do *that*." Why weren't we ever just taught to "Wish for the best of all involved," as the Universe once said in a *Note*, "and then, whatever happens, know that it was"? Then we leave room for the ideal thing to happen to the appropriate person based on their learning schedule, desired adventures, with Divine Intelligence working the logistics.

"If you want to make God laugh, tell him your plans."

Wouldn't that be galling?! Yet we hear seemingly spiritually aware people repeat this line, or versions of it, attributed to Woody Allen (among others) and stemming from a similar Yiddish proverb. This is the same as saying, "Forget about whatever it is you want, God decides everything. Just fasten your seat belt." Which is the same as disavowing *all of your power.*

Again, life is not something that happens to you, not 10 percent, not 1 percent, not any percent. YOU happen to life, 24/7 100 percent! Of course, there might seem to be a lot of laughter from the heavens, if your end results are on the right side of the Matrix—it'll work, it won't, or you'll have wished it hadn't, with no seeming rhyme or reason. Leaving you to think, as some do, *Oh, the Universe has a wicked sense of humor.* No, that was just crossed wires and micromanagement on your part. You don't have to worry about God or the angels laughing when you're on the left side of the Matrix, not that they'd laugh under any circumstances. On the left side of the Matrix, everything works more swiftly for your highest and greatest good.

"What about my new car, my commission check, my date with Trixie?"

For this last possible objection, I wanted to make it as relevant to your life today as possible. Admittedly, this Matrix-big-picture-end-results approach is pretty radical compared to all the teachers who tell you manifesting change is all about details, details, details! By the end of this book, you will have absolutely no trouble changing horses, though at first there's room for misunderstandings. This objection's "real hypotheticals" are to illustrate that you don't actually have to change much with regard to how you already define your dreams. Just a little nip and tucking.

"What about my new car, Mike?" It would seem I'm saying, "Don't visualize the new red Mercedes, that's too much detail!" But I'm not.

You might ask, "What about my commission check?" especially if you've been in sales for decades, and now it seems I'm saying, "Don't imagine a specific employer or agent tripling or quadrupling your commission check, that's micromanagement!" But I'm not.

And finally, Saturday night's your hot date with Trixie! It would seem I'm saying you shouldn't imagine the "tricks" . . . I would never.

So, what's the deal?

The six columns in the Matrix are, again, your life-artist's palette; your manifestor's palette. *You can go to any of the six columns.* Just understand what you're getting yourself into. You can go to the red column, and sometimes it'll work. Sometimes it won't. And sometimes it'll work, but you'll wish it hadn't. But, yes, you can go there. Moreover, understand in advance that even if you have success in the red column, it, alone, will not bring you happiness. The solution is simple:

Dwell on the left, dabble on the right.

For example, if you do some writing and speaking for a living (ah-hum), and you've got a specific book or gig on the near horizon, imagine that all goes supremely well. Imagine happy readers, uproarious laughter, and a standing ovation—all of which are on the right side of the Matrix. But simultaneously, realize that you are more than any one book or talk. Realize when you get that specific, there are co-creators and it's not just up to you how things go. Accordingly, if a book fails to win over the public . . . blame your readers . . . Well . . . similarly ridiculous, would be blaming yourself! Actually, don't blame anyone. Don't risk drawing erroneous conclusions based upon what your physical senses are showing you, particularly when dabbling on the right side of the Matrix. It could be the book you just wrote was your warm-up for something that will be far more popular, or it could be that it *is* the book that will rock the charts, it just needs more time, or it could be neither. Most important is that you're also dwelling on the left side of the Matrix and acting accordingly! The "acting" part to be discussed fully in Chapter 5, Taking Action.

To continue with this example, even as you dabble, imagining the right side of the Matrix working out in your great favor, simultaneously see yourself as a happy, best-selling author and highly sought-after world-class professional speaker (uh-hum). Now we're much more into the Livelihood category of the Fantastic Five, with a presumed initial thrust being your happiness.

Hold on to the big picture at all times, then dabble on the right, knowing that such micromanagement may or may not work out. Dabbling *can* maximize chances that micromanagement will work for you, but doesn't guarantee it, and more, since you're mainly on the left side of the Matrix (simultaneously), you're giving great latitude to Divine Intelligence to find other forms for your expression and success (known by you, *and unknown*), be they writing, speaking, or something heretofore un-thought of.

For Trixie, imagine joy, happiness, laughter . . . and the tricks. But don't hinge your life's happiness on Friday night, or whether or not *this* relationship even develops. Leave the door open for someone "even better." Be primarily motivated by your desire to have a great friend, travel partner, trickster, love, or whatever it is you really want, big-picture. Then, if it's Trixie, *you haven't excluded her,* you've only aided the possibility, and if it's not Trixie, the door's wide open for Bambie or Fabio, and millions of others you know not of.

Dwell on the left, dabble on the right.

GLOBAL EVENTS AND TRENDS

Earlier I mentioned we can move toward 100 percent dependability with our manifestations when using the Matrix to wisely define our end results, so long as all else mentioned herein is followed. This is because our end results will now, primarily, be of happiness and its derivatives on the left side of the Matrix. There will, however, and also rather obviously, always be certain mass global events and trends that no one person can override, unless the affected population allows them. I'm concerned, however, that by even mentioning this caveat, it might be misunderstood, and thereby become one more reason someone might give away their power, "Not my fault I haven't amassed a fortune, my spouse, family, and co-workers refuse to support me." "Not my fault I haven't found my soul mate, the world is full of idiots." So . . .

Two considerations negate such cop-outs and clarify your present power:

First, the kind of mass events and trends that could prevent a dream of yours from coming true would only be those on a massive scale, such as local currencies or economies collapsing, war, geological upheaval, health pandemics, etc. Yet even *within* these typically temporary, highly local, and undeniable rare catastrophic circumstances, there often remains the opportunity for individual and collective success and happiness.

Second, the future potential of such events and trends would have been part of the foreseeable landscape prior to this lifetime beginning. Yet still, your very birth and continued presence here today evidences that you, your higher self, or Divine Intelligence had, and still has, great plans and knows of your continued potential to flourish. Meaning, it's not by chance that you still have life, even amidst temporary, local, and rare turmoil, and of all the probable futures that now exist before you, each contains space for your overall happiness and growth. Know this, it's within you, rather than pleading hardship or handicap should the earth start shaking, shutting down your own power.

BEYOND GETTING GENERAL

Not that anything shared so far is complicated, but the following "advanced" guidelines have emerged over the many years I've been teaching the Matrix for audiences to consider when choosing and defining their end results:

1. **Be self-serving.** You can't play the Matrix for others. You can influence them, and if you've got kids or employees, this is part of your job, but nothing can ensure others will behave as you wish. When it comes to you Playing the Matrix, you must be the prime beneficiary.

2. **Your end results would ideally be so broad that
    their successful manifestation will automatically
    further the *journey* of your life, rather than just
    be destinations or stopping points.** When you
    keep your end results general, you're automatically
    choosing big-picture priority areas for change,
    the success from which will inevitably spill over
    into other large areas of your life. As opposed to
    destination end results like the car, the job title, or
    a hot date, which would only ever be a small part of
    living a rocking life.

3. **Your end results ought to make sense logically and
    feel good emotionally.** Too often spiritually aware
    people want to ditch any form of logic or intellect.
    While logic is usually overrated in our society, it
    can be a valuable tool in stirring up magic and
    possibilities, giving you new ideas of doors to knock
    upon, stones to turn over, and approaches to test.

    A hypothetical example I've used in my earlier
    works, which isn't too far from the kind of ideas I
    really do hear: "Trust me, Mike, I know about the
    law of attraction and thoughts becoming things. I
    have an idea that will revolutionize the world for
    cat lovers, while making me a fortune: kitten leg
    warmers!" As if kittens weren't already cute enough?
    "The way I see it, the Universe loves me, all things are
    possible, I'm a natural born creator, so why not? I'll
    even give you partial credit for my success, Mike."

    "Wow, that's quite an idea!" I try to glow back.
    "Kitten leg warmers . . . I never would have thought
    of that on my own." This hypothetical invention,
    however, is a lot like the person who says to me,
    "*This* [contract, book, proposal, deal, person, date,
    arrangement, or job title] is going do it for me, Mike!
    The Universe loves me. Has to work." No, it does not
    have to work; this is the kind of micromanagement

we're learning to avoid. And I wonder how much logical sense their idea really makes for them, which is the yellow flag on the play I'm talking about.

Now, who am I to say that kitten leg warmers won't be the next rage?! I don't know. But any honest resistance they or you or I might have to an idea would, at a minimum, be reflective of a limiting belief we must possess that could otherwise be sensed, if it weren't for their whitewashing it with "the Universe loves me" talk.

Limited-Belief-Busting Freebie Tip #1

If you're feeling a little bit of hesitation, logically, on a dream or a goal, it's probably an invisible, limiting, self-sabotaging belief. *Rather than looking for what's invisible*, by getting a little more logical, you can broaden the definition and scope of your desires, getting more general, until you're eventually on board with the dream. If you're having trouble intellectually believing in your kitten leg warmer idea, which I kind of hope you are, how about considering going more general, like opening a pet store online? Or maybe at a nearby shopping center or mall? How about inside your store, *in addition to kitten leg warmers*, you sell cat toys, dog leashes, and bird food? By getting a tad more logical, going down a path that is well worn with the success of others who did the same, you might have more confidence and navigate right around the invisible limiting belief creating the resistance. The beauty here is that we're fully preserving the possibilities that kitten leg warmers may be our "ticket"—nothing has been excluded. But to ward off the chance that our specificity might limit us, we've broadened the scope of the dream.

---

4. **Your end results should not be dependent on specific people, paths, and details, nor upon specific timelines.** I've already addressed the reasons for not having dreams dependent on specific people, paths, and details, so here let me address the problem with timelines, or as they are more commonly used, deadlines. As in, "I want to be a millionaire by December 31 *this year!*"

    First, I think putting deadlines on yourself is fine. I often aim to write a certain amount of words per book-writing session. What I don't recommend is putting deadlines on the Universe or life's magic. "The Universe" and "magic" are qualities we can hardly grasp with our brains, yet to be so naive at the outset of a journey as to demand your dream come true by some date on the calendar pretty much pushes the ridiculous. How can you know or demand all the details, players, and so-called coincidences, plotted on a timeline no less, necessary for your dream to come true? You simply can't, as will be scientifically shown in Chapter 4. Which isn't to deny that sometimes these deadlines pan out, if you're still okay with sometimes. I'm not.

    Second, you run the risk of shattering your own confidence with a missed deadline. For example, let's say Divine Intelligence responds silently to your demand of "millionaire by December 31" with,

    "Would love to, but your mother is about to fall sick, her rebound will depend upon certain perspectives she's learning to manage, and because of her illness, you're going to want to come clean with all that guilt and resentment you've been dragging around the past few years. Plus, you also have priorities for finding romance and your own health, remember? For all of which, I must factor and derive the perfect arrival schedules, in harmony and under grace, in this volatile world. All considered, you'll very likely have to wait no longer than the following

August 23 for your first million. Love you, mean it—The Universe"

You don't hear this. You know nothing of the changing world like the Universe does. You swear upon December 31 this year being your delivery date, burn your bridges, and fearlessly tell every living soul within ear shot of your plans and expectations.

How are you going to feel on January 1, with the same $200 in your checking account? Foolish. Embarrassed. Defeated. And how do you think these new, completely unnecessary feelings are going to affect the confidence that your fortune is, relatively, still very, very near. Very, very poorly. You'd lose confidence, feel depressed, and unwittingly give up *. . . and therefore make impossible the otherwise doable date of August 23*. Hate when that happens.

5. **Your end results should not exist solely to make other dreams come true.** Sometimes one dream coming true will help other dreams come true, as we mentioned in point 2, and that's awesome. But if you have a dream that exists *only* so that a different dream can come true, then this intermediary dream is not really a dream, it's a cleverly disguised cursed how. If you find such in your repertoire of dreams, get rid of them.

    Hypothetically, you want to live in wealth and abundance. You don't know how you're going to get there, not that you need be concerned with the hows, but after weeks of wrestling with it in your mind, you think to yourself, *I know! I'll write that book that's in me! Oprah will feature it. It'll be a bestseller. And I'll live in abundance, happily ever after.* Now you've tricked yourself into thinking that writing a book is a dream of yours, totally disregarding that you don't even like reading and that you've never written anything creative in your life. Which is not all bad; it's actually how I started.

But, if you neither have something to say, nor have a story to tell, any writing dream is inevitably a cursed how. And if this simplistic, made-up scenario actually applied to someone, they'd be well advised to drop the writing dream, *while retaining the abundance dream, which is what they really wanted.* Remember, you don't have to know how your dream will come true! The hows will work themselves out as you take action (as we'll see in Chapter 5).

It's the linkage that's the problem. If you want to dream of both, *each for valid reasons,* do so *independent of each other.* Go for both! Either are great Fantastic Five end results. You just don't want one to exist solely for making the other happen.

THE OBJECTIFICATION OF MANIFESTING CHANGE

Given my background as a certified public accountant and a left-brain-leaning intellect, I like objectification. This is probably extremely obvious by now. I also believe that through objectifying a process it's easier to learn and understand its parts and segments, again, the buttons that should be pushed and levers pulled. Hence, my creation of the Matrix. It's meant to illustrate your choices and to convey their ramifications with a quick at-a-glance view.

Nevertheless, I do understand that while the ground rules of life on Earth are objective and absolute, like "thoughts becoming things," how we play those ground rules is the epitome and joy of our subjective experience. While there are an infinite number of roads to Rome, none of those roads changes Rome. In this case, Rome isn't going anywhere; its location is objective and absolute, yet the road you take creates your subjective experience, for which there are an infinite number of possibilities. Similarly, by objectifying the rows and column in the Matrix with labels and arrows, you can see what you're dealing with, yet how you subjectively play it, where you choose to focus your attention and priorities, will become the artistic production of your life.

That said, no reader of this book needs to carry around a copy of the Matrix through the remaining days of their life. It will have already imparted a clarified understanding of what's important and what's not. How thoughts become things, and the flow of all manifestations. Once you get this, you can go on your merry way, always mindful that happiness is the ultimate end result, having priority areas for change among the Fantastic Five to help you bring about targeted transformation, knowing that you're always free to dabble on the right side now that you understand the related implications.

To round out the objectification of creating change, let me say that there are three steps to Playing the Matrix, knowing in advance that you may put shortcuts here or there, blend end results as we will do later in the book, and take whatever other roads you invent.

Steps to Playing the Matrix

1. Choose a general end result.
2. Get into the details, just don't attach to them.
3. Take action, without messing with the "hows."

That is the simplicity of our new program for living deliberately and creating consciously, and each of these steps gets a much closer look in chapters of their own that follow.

THE MATRIX

Nothing about the Matrix detracts from, nor makes more complicated, the one immovable, pivotal principle through which all manifestations arrive: Thoughts Become Things. Yet, clearly, our thoughts do not become things spontaneously. Today, post–Big

Bang, there's a momentum and continuity created by all prior individual and collective manifestations, complete and in progress. Now we must contend with an existing playing field that consists of particular people who think in particular ways. Our manifestations must be in alignment with those to be affected, as theirs must be with ourselves, at least for as long as we're in each other's lives. Happily, the world is so large, and awesome people so plentiful, that while you can't manipulate details, hows, and loved ones, you can still live your life with love, health, abundance, fulfillment, and other big-picture objectives, that will come with their own details, hows, and people. To do so, these values must be our focus, as we tone down the urge and resist the logic to meddle vis-à-vis micromanagement.

To recap some of the most important lessons concerning the Matrix:

1. The need to micromanage one's life stems from a failure to understand life's magic.

2. Wisely *defining* our dreams is a huge factor in whether they can come true.

3. By having general end results, a more effortless approach to creating change emerges.

4. All you've ever learned about living deliberately can still be used with just a few tweaks.

5. Your happiness is key to sparking great tangible and intangible changes in your life.

TRY THIS AT HOME

Understanding Your Motivation

This calls back to the first exercise, when I asked, "What's the main reason you'd like to learn how to live deliberately and create consciously?" and "Why?"

Please consider whether your earlier answer and rationale are congruent with the lessons reviewed in this chapter.

1. Are you to be the primary beneficiary of the transformation you now seek, or are you doing it for someone else? Preferably the former.

2. Does this dream's manifestation enable the journey or adventure of your life to take off? Or was it mostly a destination end result? Preferably the former.

3. Do you feel comfortable with the end result you stated in your heart and in your mind? Preferably both.

4. Does its manifestation depend on specific people, paths, details, or timelines? Preferably not.

5. Are other dreams of yours dependent on this dream first coming true? Sometimes that's okay, unless it's the only reason you have this dream, in which case this dream is merely a cursed how.

6. Was it generally stated? Ideally, it was.

In the next chapter, we'll dive into Step 1 of Playing the Matrix by seeing how easy it is to know what we want and define some new end results that better avail us of life's magic, even when we feel lost, jaded, or just plain tired of trying to figure everything out.

Chapter 3

KNOWING WHAT YOU (REALLY) WANT

Seems like *knowing what you really want* should be the easiest thing in the world, right? It's not. It may even be the most elusive, given that we get so caught up with trying to figure everything out, instead of feeling it out. Doing so, we lose touch with what we really want, sometimes confusing "it" with how we'll get it. Leading us to think things like, *I want "X" to go "this way," which will set me up for a raise at work, thereby more recognition, higher status, and more fun. To make this all happen I need to really impress Jill, who knows Mary, and they'll both be at the ball in two months. So, if I can get ACME Company to choose me as their representative, and if I buy some oh-so-impressive new shoes, that will hopefully be back in stock next week, I'll be good to go!*

Ain't it true? And such confusion is evident whenever I ask audiences to raise their hands if they've not yet figured out what they're going to be when they grow up; 80 percent don't know. And what an incredibly precarious place to be, because, after all, "You better figure it out, young lady or young man, because no one's going to figure it out for you." Ack!! And then they say, "*Go! The early bird gets the worm! Opportunity only knocks once! Make haste! Never give up!*" But how can you go anywhere if you're among the 80 percent who don't know what they'll be when they grow up? Where would you go? How do you act on that which you can't see?! And such pressures can lead to a paralysis for fear of getting it wrong.

Couple this funk with a misinterpretation of the lessons we shared in *The Secret* and, again, we hear some readers excitedly exclaim, "I don't have to figure *anything* out. Ha! Ha! La-dee-dah! There's a beautiful, doting Universe that wants for me what I want for myself . . . ah-h! Silly that I ever worried!" And so, they passively wait for their path to appear . . . forever. We do need to take action, we must. But the trick, again, is realizing that it doesn't matter what we do as much as it does that we're doing something, to the best of our seemingly feeble ability, to move in the direction of our dreams. Of course, we'll talk lots about giving yourself direction, later; that's step three of Playing the Matrix. For now, this chapter is about knowing what you really want, defined wisely. Step 1 of sparking transformation.

MY PARALYSIS

As a Boy

I can relate to the confusion that's born of desire mingled with uncertainty. Can't everyone?

My first bout came at age five. I remember Mom used to take my four-year-old sister, Amanda, and me to our favorite treat of all treats, if we had been good . . . forever. It was a little coin-operated merry-go-round at the far end of the mall. Two little ponies that revolved around a pole. I loved this little drill; my sister and I thought the two ponies were racing, and invariably I would be in the lead. (Yeah, she thought she was winning each race, too.)

I remember my last visit to that little ride. We had been dutiful all morning while Mom shopped for boring stuff. And finally, it was our turn. She set us free. We ran like little kids run, across the mall, sliding up to our steeds. Amanda was on first. While I had one leg in the air, one still on the ground, suddenly I saw my pony in a new light. I could no more bring myself to get all the way on than I could get all the way off and run away—both of which I wanted to do. Mom caught up: "Mike, honey. What's wrong?" "Mom . . . *it's stupid!*" I suddenly saw it as a plastic pony that went nowhere, in a race no one wins! But . . . if I turned my back on it, on a treat that had on so many occasions brought me great joy, then what would replace it? Without even articulating the revelations sweeping my mind, Mom saw right through me as she always could. "Oh, Mike, honey. It's okay. This just means you're growing up. There's going to be other stuff. Better stuff, I promise."

But when you're trained to interpret reality with your physical senses alone, in a world that knows nothing of your spiritual, inner nature, and *when you can't see what's next*, it's hard to know if *anything's* even there. Right? Much less have faith in it, much less act on it! Paralysis.

Mom was right. Other fun stuff came along. And later, I remember, as all kids must, being asked, "What are you going to be when you grow up?" As long as you have an answer (mine were "fireman, policeman, astronaut") everybody's happy. When you don't have an answer, no matter your age, 7 or 70, it's as if alarm bells sound: "Oh, Mike! Sheelagh, little Mike doesn't know what he's going to be when he grows up. Mike, don't you know you can be anything? Anything you want?" "That's the problem!" Too many choices. Along with the implication you could choose wrong! Every year the world changes so much. Wouldn't it be a travesty, we reason, if we chose poorly? What if next year the Internet goes in a whole new direction, making your own career path crystal clear. Maybe you should just wait and see what happens . . .

As a Man

Despite my fun answers as a boy, I grew up to become a certified public accountant. Which, of course, was my choice, and frankly was a great thing for six years. Until I wanted more. And not knowing what that "more" would be, how it would take form, or if it even existed, I finally decided to force the answer by quitting my job at Price Waterhouse without knowing what would come next. Suddenly the funk was back on. This time I was 29 years old, without the self-confidence that came with working for a prestigious global firm, struggling to define myself to the world, including to a landlord at an apartment complex in Orlando, which seemed so beneath me after being a homeowner in Boston. "Name and where you work, please." "Um . . . I'm figuring that out right now." Even my new local bank wanted to know who my employer was. I started telling some questioners I was actually retired, thank you very much. Great shock value when you're saying this at 29 years of age. But for a very long time I secretly wondered if I had just made the biggest mistake of my life, leaving the firm and a salary that in today's dollars would be into six figures. Paralysis.

> Humbled, desperate, and once again in a fear-induced paralysis, I remember getting on my knees and praying before bed at night, "Dear God . . ."

For months, unemployed, I snooped around for business opportunities, looking into franchises, attending fairs and tradeshows, and reading *Fortune*, *Forbes*, and similar magazines for inspiration. Nothing turned up. Meanwhile, my brother had several freelance jobs working at Universal Studios in film production, and was simultaneously receiving monthly royalty payments of over $1,000 for T-shirt designs he had created back in art school! Fortunately, while I was green with envy, Mom had a vision, and she urged, nagged, and begged us to incorporate our own T-shirt company: "Mike, you're the accountant, Andy, the designer . . . and I'll join you doing whatever I can to help!" Can't really argue with Mom.

After a wickedly slow start, our little T-shirt company went global and had a great run. By the tenth year, however, as trends were declining, we liquidated to avoid going out of business. Ugh! *I'm starting over again?! What happened? I'm almost 40 years old, and I have no career momentum? I'm starting over . . . and I don't even know what I'm starting?*

People talk about having no light at the end of their tunnel. I had no tunnel. I did have, however, enough money to coast for two years. But my mortgage was many times larger than my savings. So, I worried and wondered if the best of my time on Earth was actually behind me, with seemingly nothing (that I could see with my physical senses) in front of me. I was truly scared for my life.

I would lose sleep each night, bathed in sweat, for two reasons: 1) My life's predicament. 2) Not allowing myself to run my home air conditioner, in Orlando, Florida, under 82 degrees for fear of burning through my life savings. Tossing and turning, I'd wonder, *What did I do, that I shouldn't have done, that could have avoided this seeming catastrophe in my life? Or, what didn't I do, that I should have done, that could have avoided this nightmare?* I remember thinking (I'm embarrassed to admit), *Maybe this is the way my life was supposed to go* (as if some things were predetermined, not). I had a great run at PW. Another selling T-shirts where Mom, Andy, and I sold over a million of them! By 39 I'd already traveled to dozens of countries. How am I ever going to top all that? *Maybe . . . now I'm supposed to see how other people live.* This was also at a time I found out my girlfriend (*another* one) had a boyfriend, and he wasn't me.

Humbled, desperate, and once again in a fear-induced paralysis, I remember getting on my knees and praying before bed at night, "Dear God . . ." (Ever notice how when feeling happy we say "the Universe" or "Source" or "Divine Intelligence," but when scared, it's "Dear God"?) *"DEAR GOD!"* I prayed, *"I have no idea* how I've created the mess I'm in, but *I know what I want!* I want enough money to not worry about losing my home (and then some). I want to have a rocking career, although I have no idea what that might be." I'd already worn the hat of corporate America with PW, and then the hat of an entrepreneur selling T-shirts for 10 years, and neither one of them was calling me back. "I want to live the rest of my life surrounded by friends and laughter. And I want to start traveling again, internationally, please." Granted, travel might seem indulgent, yet for both my accounting and T-shirt years I was frequently abroad, and . . . it was *my* prayer. Those were my wishes:

1. wealth and abundance

2. creative, fulfilling work

3. friends and laughter, and

4. traveling internationally, again.

And I most distinctly remember punctuating that prayer with a rather abrupt, if not annoyed, "*You* figure it out!" Not that I was angry at God. I was angry at myself for feeling so helpless.

LO AND BEHOLD, A MASTER PLAN EMERGES

Do you notice a common trait among my four desires? It's not obvious, but if you think back to one of the columns in the Matrix, something might strike you.

They're *generally* stated . . . Whoa! Not that I had *any idea* of what I was doing at the time. It most certainly wasn't because I was clever. I was desperate and scared, having micromanaged the heck out of everything up until then, which at the time had seemed the most effective way to live deliberately. I had already worn all the hats that seemed to suit me, but they no longer fit! I couldn't think of what else to ask "God" for, in terms of details, so by accident, not knowing any better, at the end of my micromanaging rope, I got general!

> Talk about pressure— we've carried the weight of the world on our shoulders! Why? Because we've confused the means with the end; the hows for our dreams!

Step 1 of Playing the Matrix—go "big picture"!

In the days and weeks that followed my nightly bedside prayers, I instinctively knew (as do we all) that I had to maintain some sense of optimism and buoyancy. How might one do this? Vision boards! Reading favorite empowering books kept on my nightstand! Creative visualization! Fun pictures stuck on my refrigerator! Using affirmations! All the tools that are likely known and used by the typical reader of this book, and if that's not you, in Chapter 6 I'll give you lots of ideas. Maintaining optimism and buoyancy is essentially *Step 2 of Playing the Matrix—getting into the details!*

In those same days and weeks, I also instinctively knew (as do we all) that if I wanted my life rescued, I had to show up in the world and take action. Get out of the house. Doing anything is better than doing nothing. Just like when I moved from Boston to Orlando, I snooped around for business opportunities— looked into franchises, attended fairs and tradeshows, updated my résumé, and again read *Fortune, Forbes*, and similar magazines, this time looking for business opportunities. I asked friends and acquaintances for help and guidance, knocked on doors, turned over stones, and rustled the bushes. Showing up and taking action is essentially *Step 3 of Playing the Matrix—go, now, never stop!*

I knew nothing of this game plan that was emerging day by day or that I was even following one, other than my approach seemed pure common sense. Nothing was unique about it, *other than Step 1, having general end results*, which was simply a function of having exhausted my known list of options. My Steps 2 and 3 were things to do that are covered in virtually all self-improvement books or courses, nevertheless, I'll continue my story, including how I took those next two steps in terms of the Matrix, in the next two chapters.

YOU HAD IT ALL ALONG

And so, we're getting to the point of this chapter. Who doesn't want "abundance, fun, friends, and travel"? And what might be another, grander, more all-encompassing word that likely implies each of these for most people? *Happiness?* Yes, happiness! And who doesn't want happiness?

Did you really need me to tell you what you really want is happiness? I'm afraid so, because your entire life, you and everyone else have been urged to turn the question of "What do I want?" into "How am I going to get there?"! And thereby, we've come to believe we don't even know what we want, when we actually do, thinking instead that we have to answer the question of "How?" with a sexy-cool career that will thrill us and make all else possible. We even sheepishly think we're already supposed to be rocking this sexy-cool vocation, except we don't know what it is yet! Paralysis.

You've always known what you wanted, "Happiness!" but you've been taught it's something you have to achieve, doing what you love, instead of being shown it's about loving what you do and seeing where it leads. Neither have we been taught we can feel happiness now, for no reason. And given that most of our "achieving" in life comes from our careers, it's been implied that to be successful (happy), we have to make wise choices, find our sacred, birth-destined niche, invoke divine intervention, perform clutch plays, get a little lucky, and shed copious amounts of blood, sweat, and tears. Talk about pressure—we've carried the weight of the world on our shoulders! Why? Because we've confused the means with the end; the hows for our dreams!

WHAT IT REALLY MEANS TO GROW UP

In the early days of delivering the Matrix, I'd occasionally hear from the accomplished audience member, who was often advanced in years, who'd say something like, "You know, Mike, I get it. I've been living this Matrix, thoughts become things, my whole life without realizing what I was doing, but Mike . . . you need to create a program for those of us who no longer know where our passions lie, who've already worn all the hats, been there, done that." And I tell them, as Mom once told me, "It's okay. This just means you're growing up. There's going to be other stuff. There's going to be better stuff, I promise." To which I add, "And you'll find it so much quicker once you stop dwelling on the right-hand side of the Matrix, concerned about the 'cursed hows.'" Which, of course, is exactly where they are when they're trying to logistically figure out and micromanage *how* they will one day be happy again.

Understand this and you'll move yourself from a state of understandable confusion into one of crystal-clear clarity. For example, while 80 percent of every adult audience, the world over, struggles with what they will be when they grow up, watch how the question marks turn into excited exclamation points when we slide just one column over to the left on the Matrix, from right to left.

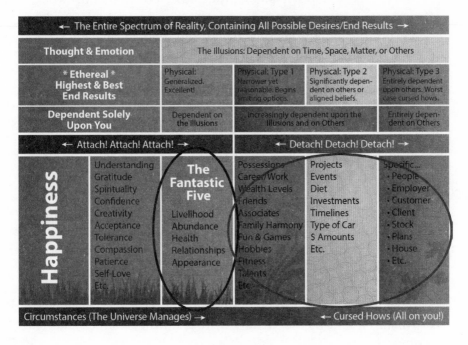

← The Entire Spectrum of Reality, Containing All Possible Desires/End Results →				
Thought & Emotion	The Illusions: Dependent on Time, Space, Matter, or Others			
* Ethereal * **Highest & Best** **End Results**	Physical: Generalized. Excellent!	Physical: Type 1 Narrower yet reasonable. Begins limiting options.	Physical: Type 2 Significantly dependent on others or aligned beliefs.	Physical: Type 3 Entirely dependent upon others. Worst case cursed hows.
Dependent Solely **Upon You**	Dependent on the Illusions	Increasingly dependent upon the Illusions and on Others		Entirely dependent on Others
← Attach! Attach! Attach! →		← Detach! Detach! Detach! →		
Happiness	Understanding Gratitude Spirituality Confidence Creativity Acceptance Tolerance Compassion Patience Self-Love Etc.	**The Fantastic Five** Livelihood Abundance Health Relationships Appearance	Possessions Career/Work Wealth Levels Friends Associates Family Harmony Fun & Games Hobbies Fitness Talents Etc.	Projects Events Diet Investments Timelines Type of Car $ Amounts Etc.	Specific... • People • Employer • Customer • Client • Stock • Plans • House • Etc.
Circumstances (The Universe Manages) →			← Cursed Hows (All on you!)	

Figure 3.1

For example, is there any doubt in your mind that Abundance might not fit your future lifestyle? Maybe Health isn't all that it's been cracked up to be? Not sure that you even want a livelihood, great friends, and to be happy about your appearance? Ha! You know, times six (the Fantastic 5 plus Happiness)! You know the answer to what you're going to be when you grow up, inside and out, with total confidence and clarity. We're all born knowing what we want, it's just that our entire lives we've been led astray by well-meaning people who have been telling us, "Yeah, well you better figure out how, Buck-o." Wrong! Worst advice ever!

The great irony, of course, is that those who don't know what they're going to be when they grow up are in an awesome place (unless they are choosing to feel bad about it). By not knowing the right side of the Matrix—the hows—you free up infinite possibilities for the Universe to connect these dots for you.

Incidentally, if you're among the 20 percent who know what they want, let the rest of this chapter serve as confirmation to what your life has already shown you, and then, in Chapter 5, I'll have a very important lesson intended specifically for you on the topic of diversification.

HOW NOT TO BE YOUR OWN WORST CRITIC

If your goals and dreams are too "close" in terms of time or space, in other words, if you're trying to micromanage your success, you're likely to shoot them down almost as soon as you prop them up. Why? Because you can be your own worst critic, and with goals or dreams that near, you'll already know lots of reasons they might not work out.

For example, let's say you're a realtor, and after being particularly inspired for whatever reason, you wake up one morning feeling like king or queen of the universe! You visualize, meditate, or whatever, and then you start writing down some new short-term goals.

This year:

I'm going to list four times as many homes as I did last year!

I'm going to close on all of them!

I'm going to start expanding my territory!

I might even get my broker's license!

I give you about two days, before you start wondering, like you often do, if you should even be in real estate. "Why did I get into sales to begin with? I hate sales! I don't even know if we're entering a buyer's market or a seller's market."

On the other hand, let's hypothetically say you're the same inspired realtor, but in this example when you start writing down some new short-term goals, they sound like this.

This year:

The floodgates of abundance are about to start trembling!

I will discover myself and my gifts as I move into clarity!

I will absolutely love all that I do; it will feel like play!

My friendship circles will expand and my business connections will multiply!

(These statements would be even more potent if written in the present [or past] tense, as if they were already true. A concept that'll be reviewed in Chapter 6.)

This latter list of goals, *being far more general*, is also far more difficult to argue. Right? Why not? Why wouldn't the floodgates begin to tremble? Why wouldn't you discover yourself, have clarity, love what you do, and have lots more connections? By going "big picture," we greatly diminish our own ability to shoot our dreams down. That's all you've ever had to do. That's what you're "supposed" to do. Micromanagement be gone. Later, you can get excited about these generalities by getting into the details. But in this chapter, all we want are end results that will later avail us of life's magic, as we show up in the world.

HOW TO AVOID MAKING BIG DECISIONS

One of life's seeming necessities, and burdens, is having to make big decisions that may well affect the rest of our days. Wouldn't you love to be absolved of this responsibility? Wouldn't you like for there to be a system in place that chooses the best and highest and most loving answer for you? Or to be so evolved your-self, that you can see, with supreme confidence, the direction you should go? No matter the looming fork in the road of your life, never having to doubt your choice, second-guess your intuition, or consider quitting? Can you imagine? Sound far-fetched? Impossible? It's not. This is real. Those days of anguish and fear can be left behind for good, when you simply name what you want in grand, bold, general terms.

> **The Universe is loving and lenient. It allows for massive wiggle room.**

This lesson was exemplified by a questioner in my audience many years ago (I'll change some facts to preserve his identity), when he asked, "Mike, at what point might it be okay to let go of something you've been pursuing for a long time? Is that quitting on a dream? Is it ever okay to quit on a dream? Is it ever okay to conclude it isn't 'meant to be'?" Immediately, I wanted to shout, "Never give up! Never give . . ." But I hesitated. Yikes! There are those nuances and the Bermuda Triangle of Mani-festing . . . What if someone's dream had landed there? Is hinged on a specific person behaving a specific way? Expecting a cursed how to be their comeback story? Depends upon an unimportant detail—all details being unimportant? In which case, they started their journey out on a very slippery slope! And the sooner they get off that slope, the better. Right?

The questioner continued, "I'm on my third home mortgage, and spent every penny I had ever saved on an invention that I'm really proud of. The patent is now pending in Washington, D.C." That's a green light. A really good thing. "The problem is, I've manufactured a couple thousand of these gizmos, which are like tools, or toys, that make learning fun. They're so simple that chil-dren can use them to do their homework. So effective, that par-ents can use them too, whether for continuing educations, going back to school, or to help learn a new language." The questioner really lit up when he pointed out that his invention was a great way to increase family time if parents used it to help their kids with their homework!

"My friends think it's a great idea!" Your friends will think that. "But now I have 2,000 of them in my garage, beautifully made in the Orient, collecting dust. I've placed a few on consignment in retail stores," which means they're not paid for until sold, "but consumers don't quite 'get it.' If I only had $10,000 more, I could invest in merchandise display units that would educate consumers on the fly about the virtues of my gizmo. But I don't. I'm behind on mortgage payments and I might lose my home."

Hence the question, "Is it ever okay to give up on a dream?" After a quick panic, I turned to the Matrix.

Which column would you say this patent-pending device might be in? Let's be generous. Second in from the right? It's like a Project. And the reason this person is in this dilemma, having invested everything—time, energy, livelihood—into this gizmo, was their original, motivating thought, *Boy, when this thing grows wings, I'm going to be swimming in appreciation, adventure, and abundance. My livelihood will be rocking, I'll be the talk of the town and the happiest person alive.* A classic cursed-how approach. All eggs in one basket, beginning on the right, because theoretically, they think it's *how* they'll become happy.

So, with the little I knew of my questioner's situation, I suggested that if we were starting over, "Instead of beginning on the right side of the Matrix, what if we made happiness your main driver, while giving livelihood and abundance high priorities too?" Then, when it comes to taking action in the blue and yellow columns, we'll consider, "Given this equation, what doors might I knock on? What paths might I choose?" (Real examples of taking action on the right side of the Matrix based upon similar end results will be shared in Chapter 5.)

One of those doors should definitely be his impassioned idea for the patent-pending invention. But I would rarely advocate doing that one thing, and *nothing* else! Contrary to what others might advise, like "Stake your claim, burn your bridges, and never give up!" Who needs the drama? Why risk your health, your sanity, or the roof over your head? The Universe is loving and lenient. It allows for massive wiggle room. Knock on that door, but simultaneously knock on others, because you just can't know how your dream will come true, and it just might *not* be through your patent-pending gizmo.

Given this person's revealed passion for kids, education, and family time, let's go there for more doors to knock upon. He might also:

1. Create a website and Internet presence representing these topics.

2. Write about his ideas on a blog.

3. Invent a board game that could also serve as a learning tool.

4. Send out "Notes from My Gizmo."

5. Write a nonfiction book on the virtues of learning at all ages that briefly references the Gizmo.

6. Write a kid's book extolling learning and family time that also briefly references the Gizmo.

7. Become a professional speaker, teaching about the virtues of lifelong learning.

8. Become a life coach addressing these values that are so important to him.

9. Work for a large organization that already caters to children, families, and/or learning—to better understand the trade, make contacts, and get ideas for his own future company.

Here are nine paths or doors to consider, among many more that only the questioner could know, *for this one passion that we know of!* Surely, like for all of us, our questioner has a few more areas of interest. Maybe management? Maybe human resources? Maybe gardening and horticulture? Maybe sales and marketing? Consider then, knocking on the same nine doors, *for each of his other interest areas!* Suddenly, instead of one door for his gizmo, there are 45 doors!

A Note from the Universe

What if the word *work* was changed to *dance-with-life*? And instead of it being viewed as an alternative to fishing or a way of "paying your dues," it was seen as a chance to meet a parade of new friends, discover your own untested potentials and unpolished gifts, and create the chance for miracles to come pouring into your life?

Yeah, I bet lottery sales would plummet.

Start the parade,
The Universe

P.S. Not to mention the office parties, donut runs,
paychecks, and "free" pens . . . Cha, cha, cha!

Try them all out. Simultaneously, if you can. See what gives. What feels right. Where is there resistance? If at any point one of those doors is proving fruitless, driving you crazy, no more fun to knock on, or is risking your health, sanity, and roof over your head, STOP KNOCKING ON *THAT* DOOR!

Now, with 45 other irons in the fire, if you take one out, is that quitting or giving up? Ha! No. We're moving with our end result of happiness and priorities of livelihood and abundance. We're just going to give one of the doors a little rest, or a long rest. This is what it means to never have to doubt, second-guess, or quit, because you're being driven by happiness; if you're alive and your end results are on the left side of the Matrix, the game is forever on.

For instance, at what point in anyone's life journey would it be reasonable to give up on or let go of their happiness? Their finances? Their health? Their friendships? Such questions are so ridiculous, they never come up. We never even consider them. And neither will you ever have to doubt or second-guess again when you realize what your real goal is, the ultimate end result, your happiness, for which there is always more one can do. And by all means, have other end results, too. Other priority areas that you're also focused on, that you're dressing up on vision boards, and that you're taking baby steps toward. Life is not about having one dream at a time, unless that dream is happiness. Life is about living a grand and full adventure on all fronts.

As long as you're still doing stuff, it's still happening, it's still working out. Hence, it's impossible to fail, because you're always in the go mode. And once you're a bit down the path, as you'll hear later, it gets easier and easier, to such a degree, that the last thing you'd ever want to do is stop. When you understand life's mechanics, it becomes more like a game. Playing is fun. It's better than a video game. The main point being, once your end results are general, the only big decisions you have to make, other than to focus on your happiness, is where your priority areas are for change.

KNOWING WHAT YOU (REALLY) WANT

Consider, Divine Intelligence sees all and knows all. So, when you give it a big-picture end result like a rocking career, great relationships, or happiness, it silently replies, "Oh! That's easy. You live in an illusionary world with seven and a half billion co-creators. You think 'this,' believe 'that,' love 'the other.' You're great with people, challenged by numbers . . . got it! I'm all over it! *Consider it done!*"

The simple lessons from this Step 1 of Playing the Matrix can be summarized like this:

1. You already know exactly what you want, when you keep it general.

2. When you keep it general, you shoot past your own known objections.

3. When your end results are general, you never have to doubt, second-guess, or quit—failure becomes impossible.

4. The more general your end results, the faster and easier they'll manifest.

5. Let your highest life priorities for change help you choose where to begin.

TRY THIS AT HOME

What are your highest priority areas for change or transformation today?

Ask yourself this incredibly simple question. It's much easier to answer than having to declare to the world, "This is who I will be when I grow up!" Immediately, instinctively, we know where our highest priorities for change are when generally stated. And this is what Step 1 of Playing the Matrix is all about—knowing in a big-picture sense where your highest priority areas are for sparking transformation in your life.

For me, they were wealth and abundance; creative, fulfilling work; friends and laughter; and international travel. So, keeping general and working on the left side of the Matrix, *creatively phrase up to five—you really only need one for direction—*of your most prized end results, choosing words that suit you or feel free to use my own.

Here are some examples of possible word combinations that may help you make this exercise more personal and playful, to show how you might frame what you want, rather than blandly stating, "I want a better livelihood," which doesn't sound so alluring.

- Rock my school/studies!
- Love my healthy, sexy body!
- Be creatively fulfilled!
- Look and feel slim & gorgeous!
- Have a vibrant social life!
- Be surrounded by friends and laughter!

- Date often, wisely, and well!
- I am a highly sought-after expert in my field!
- Flourishing, happy family time!

- Have loads of free, creative time!
- Be happier! Have fun! Play often!
- Become spiritually alive and joyfully enlightened!

1st Area to transform: _____

_____

_____

2nd Area to transform: _____

_____

_____

3rd Area to transform: _____

_____

_____

4th Area to transform: _____

_____

_____

5th Area to transform: _____

_____

_____

A Note from the Universe

Bees can fly 12 miles without getting lost. Albatrosses, 25,000 miles. And flying insects, without eyes, have no trouble whatsoever finding their "soul mates."

Imagine what I can do for you when you stop worrying about the hows and begin listening to the voice within.

Tallyho,
The Universe

P.S. Voice, not voices.

Playing the Matrix has three steps. We just did Step 1. Easy. Your homework is to always be aware of your changing priorities. As we grow and evolve, so do our tastes and preferences, and there's no shame in changing our minds or even shedding old visions of what we used to think we wanted. Feel free to modify and edit your end results as time goes by, yet know that for at least having them you give yourself direction for Steps 2 and 3, to follow.

We all want happiness and most of the exact same big-picture values. In Steps 2 and 3 of Playing the Matrix, however, you'll see how you can "dress up" and act on the same end results (as other people), yet in very different, totally unique ways.

Chapter 4

GETTING INTO
THE DETAILS

The second step of Playing the Matrix, we said, is to "Get into the details, *just DON'T attach to them.*" Having taught this for many years now, I know it brings up immediate resistance. "How can you do both at the same time? Doesn't getting into the details foster attachment?"

No, not any more than watching a movie with your favorite actor or actress implies you'll be a stalker. Not any more than reading a book about mystery, promiscuity, or murder implies you are a deviant. Not any more than having a great time with a friend means you want to always be at their side. It's easy to go on, I'll spare you.

Through understanding, all things become clear. So, if we truly understand this step about the details and nonattachment, *really understand it*, it will become impossible to get into them AND attach. To do so, just keep in mind that the objective of this step is to generate excitement, passion, and emotion for our otherwise general, vague, and possibly boring end results, by imagining all the fun *types* of details that will soon be added to our lives for the transformation that's coming.

A Note from the Universe

You don't have to understand all that happens, figure out every twist in the plot, or even know why the winds sometimes blow as they do, to grasp that I do, I have, and that ultimately, each and every story has a fairy-tale ending.

I wasn't born under a truck, you know.
The Universe

WHY TWO STEPS FOR THE GPS ANALOGY
BUT THREE FOR PLAYING THE MATRIX

Step one for any GPS adventure is setting your destination, which geographically must be extremely precise, right down to a single street address that very likely does not exist anywhere else on the planet. If we did the same, however, for Step 1 of Playing the Matrix, it would inevitably ensnare specific people, and/or a specific "how," and/or specific details, landing us in the Bermuda Triangle of Manifestation. The workaround is super simple: Let Step 1 for Playing the Matrix be general, thereby allowing Divine Intelligence to find exactly the right people, hows, and details from a far greater pool of possibilities than if you were specific.

Consider, however, that paramount for making your thoughts become things is a strong emotional charge behind those thoughts. The greater the emotion around a wisely defined end result, the faster its manifestation. Ideally, then, when you think about your end results, you'd simultaneously ooze passion, joy, gratitude, appreciation, and excitement for them. Except now, with general, likely vague end results, such emotion might be far more difficult to evoke. Hence, the new, super-simple step for Playing the Matrix that does not exist for the GPS analogy is *Step 2, get into the details, just don't attach to them.*

Step 2 of the GPS analogy then becomes Step 3 of Playing the Matrix. Done.

Steps for a New Adventure

GPS Navigation	Playing the Matrix
Step 1 – Set precise destination.	Step 1 – Set general destination.
Step 2 – Put car in gear and go!	Step 2 – Get into the juicy details.
	Step 3 – Take action and go!

It's this new middle step that's the point of this chapter. The reason we're now adding details to the equation is simple—to incite emotion. *Nonattachment* to those details then becomes the only issue.

THE MADNESS OF ATTACHMENT

Rather than speak to the grades and shades of attachment, I'd rather show you, in a crystal-clear, scientific fashion, the *utter futility* of insisting upon the "who, what (details), where, and when" of your dreams. Because, as I was saying, when you really, at a core level, *get* something—when you really understand something—your insights will immediately free you from prior unhelpful, repeating loops of behavior and unpleasant experiences.

Have you heard of chaos theory?

Chaos theory is a branch of mathematics focused on the behavior of certain *systems in motion* that give the impression of random activity, even though these systems are deterministic. More simply, scientists have found systems in nature—like the weather, genetics being passed to offspring, branches sprouting off of tree trunks—that appear to be random, yet at the end of the day, or season, or millennia, patterns emerge that could have, in fact, been anticipated with total, absolute confidence. In other words, scientists have found systems from which *they can't know what's going to happen next*, yet overall, big picture, these same systems have clearly identifiable, fully anticipated, projectable end results! Yes, sounds like something we've been talking about . . .

> When you really, at a core level, *get* something— when you really understand something— your insights will immediately free you from prior unhelpful, repeating loops of behavior and unpleasant experiences.

Indeed, just because you don't know *how* your dream will come true, nor with who, when, where, etc., *this doesn't jeopardize the confidence you can otherwise have (assuming it was on the left side of the Matrix) that it will come true!*

CHAOS THEORY IN ACTION

Twenty or thirty years ago, I saw a documentary on Public Broadcasting Service television showing how scientists at University of California – Santa Cruz found chaos in a dripping water faucet. What they witnessed was re-created for viewers in three video clips that I will describe, including the insights gained:

The Drip – A non-chaotic sequence

This shot of a kitchen faucet was of a steady, consistent dripping. The size of the water drops was unchanging, the time interval between the drops was unchanging. Know these values, they said, and you could easily, confidently calculate exactly how much water would drip into the sink below on an hourly basis, and this number would never change, hour after hour, year after year, so long as the initial parameters didn't change.

Got it? Simple. No tricks here. This sequence did not illustrate chaos, but it will help you understand it by the third video.

The Gush – A non-chaotic sequence

This shot showed a steady, consistent gushing from a fully opened tap. The rate of flow was unchanging. The diameter of the stream was unchanging. The ratio of water to air bubbles was unchanging. Know these values, they said, and you could easily, confidently calculate exactly how much water would gush into the sink below on an hourly basis, and this number would never change, hour after hour, year after year, so long as the initial parameters didn't change.

Again, simple. No tricks. Similarly, this sequence did not illustrate chaos, but it too will help you understand it in the next video.

Chaos in Action

The final clip was of a sight you've no doubt seen in your own home many times. It was of the same faucet, but now the water was in between a steady drip and an open gush, creating an unpredictable, messy dribbling. There were alternating and varying drips of unpredictable amounts. For example, a double drip followed by a triple, followed by a double, followed by a single . . . quadruple, triple, double, quadruple, single, triple, quadruple, quadruple, and on and on and on. Chaos!

Two things knocked the socks off the scientists who first grasped what they were seeing:

1. No matter how long this chaotic drip continued, it was clear that never, not in a trillion years, would a pattern emerge. Like the number pi, with trailing digits that never create a pattern, ever. It's not hard to know what drip will follow, *it's impossible!* It's not calculable. No one knows. *"God" doesn't know!*

2. Nevertheless, in spite of the clear and utterly chaotic dribbling, at the end of every hour, on the hour, *exactly the same amount of water was added to the sink below!* Let that sink in (no pun intended).

Astounding! Shocking! Impossible! Chaos! And it exists throughout nature! Now you understand why no meteorologist will ever be sure if it's going to rain tonight: *It's not knowable!* Sure, like in life, there are probabilities, but not destinies.

> **Do you see? All manifestations come to pass through the crack in our illusions, now known as chaos theory!**

Interestingly, the broader, *more general*, you get in terms of any prediction (e.g., inches of rainfall in the next month, year, decade, century) the greater your odds of success in predicting an occurrence, just like when it comes to achieving goals and manifesting dreams, the more general you get, without micromanagement, the more inevitable. Inevitable for dreams—not weather—because unlike the weather, for which there are co-creators, when it comes to your own successes, fortunes, and happiness, you are their sole creator. Do you see, unlike other manifestations of chaos, when it comes to your life, you have a say, you can dream, you can act, you can prepare the way, and then chances of your success go through the roof (so long as you're not in the Bermuda Triangle of Manifesting on the right side of the Matrix)!

No one, not even Divine Intelligence, can know *how* a dream will come true with seven and half billion co-creators, all changing their minds about what they want or loathe on the fly, creating trends, currencies, and economies, rising and falling, lefting and righting. But while no one can know how your dreams will come true, *you can still know that they will when you incorporate the simple concepts and instructions in this book.* You live in a holographic universe, smoke and mirrors. Matter is not matter. Everything is affected by your thoughts. And so long as you're not tangling with these nuances of manifestation, have general end results that you consistently act on, you will become totally unstoppable—just look at others in the world who have! Now you know why, even if they don't.

IT'S THROUGH THE CRACKS THAT THE LIGHT GETS IN

Leonard Cohen, legendary singer-songwriter, penned the lyrics in "Anthem," one of his greatest hits, that spoke to everything, no matter how seemingly perfect, having a crack in it. Which, of course, seems to imply that everything is imperfect, yet in the following line of that song, he adds, "That's how the light gets in." Gorgeous. He turned it 360 degrees. Perhaps he was saying it's through our imperfections that we are truly perfect, but I'd like to seize a tangent here and explore whether the crack in time and space is their illusionary nature, through which magic can then appear in our lives.

It sure seems so, right? Solids are not even solid . . . Time is relative . . . Thoughts become things . . . Life unfolds based upon our individual and collective focus . . . We are happening to it, it is not happening to us! *Nothing* is as it seems. This is what makes chaos possible, *through which* there are then new possibilities for creation in every moment of time. Without it, everything and every life would be predictable, unadventurous, and not even worth living! Do you see? All manifestations come to pass through the crack in our illusions, now known as chaos theory!

There's got to be room for the light, *the unexpected (but not unthought-of)*, to get in. And if the whole world didn't have this little "wobble" to it, everything would be unyielding and absolute. Do we get to see this crack? No! *That would ruin everything.* You see perfection, flow, order, making it all seem so real. Just like in a cinematic movie, do you notice every time the scenes change? From full frontal, to profile, and closer still, now peering into the eye of your heartthrob, the music reaching a crescendo . . . you don't even hear the music, yet its increased pace is pushing you to the edge of your seat! Just like you don't see the crack, until, with hindsight, you marvel over the "miracles" laden in the trails you've tread! Without chaos, the magic wouldn't be able to bring about change and transformation in the most unpredictable, even unimaginable (to us) of ways, as it always does, when you least expect it, yielding a manifestation of what you were earlier dreaming of!

HOW CHAOS WORKS IN EVERY MANIFESTATION

In Your GPS Car

Let's say you're driving down the road in your GPS-directed car and the little display monitor built into your car's dashboard is showing your location and immediate terrain (nearby roads, waterways, and other surrounding features). There's also either an arrow or car caricature designating your position in relation to all else pictured. The faster you drive, the faster the scenery flies by on your monitor. Come to a stop, it stops. Drive off the road, it drives off the road (trust me). There's also two numerical figures shown, one represents the distance you still have to go before arriving at your programmed destination, the other shows your estimated time of arrival, and all of this data is constantly being adjusted based upon *what you choose to do (as reflected in your GPS position).*

There's a *recalculation* every nanosecond of your journey between where you then are, where you want to go, and what you're presently doing, thanks to the satellite signals. Just like the Universe, Divine Intelligence knows exactly where you are every instant of every day.

Your job, at the outset of any new adventure, is twofold: 1) hold the vision of the end result you're after, and 2) keep rolling, car in gear, even when, especially when, it seems like nothing's happening. You do your part and then the Universe does the rest. As you're getting closer and driving faster, *recalculation.* Slowing down, moving off course, *recalculation.* Change your mind, slam on the brakes, *recalculation.*

Now, what happens when on your way to a new best friend's house you have a "Dunkin' Donuts Attack," and you pull off the highway to drive three miles off course to the nearest shop? The instant you deviate from your designated path, guidance is forthcoming: "Make a legal U-turn!" Just a moment ago, you were 23 miles to your originally intended destination, now it's 24 miles, now it's 25 . . . *recalc . . . recalc . . . recalc . . .* "Make a legal U-turn!" But, for having changed your mind, for pulling off course, never is the ultimate end result in jeopardy, as long as it remains an intention and you ultimately plan to get back on track. Right? And, in life, no matter how many times you change your mind, or how many different doors you knock on, or how many varying priorities you have, the Universe responds, "I know how. I still know how. I really know how." As it begins coaxing and nudging you back on point.

Let's now say, still at Dunkin' Donuts, you become very thirsty. "Starbucks Attack!" So, you head five more miles off your originally charted course, *recalc . . . recalc . . . recalc . . . recalculation.* Then, still on the way to Starbucks, in the exact right moment, on a very precise point in the highway, instead of making a legal U-turn, it now tells you to continue onward to the next traffic light, to make a right, and then a left, and then right, to get to your originally scheduled destination. Suddenly, it's now faster for you to be rerouted an entirely new way to your original destination than to go back the way you came. "I know where you are . . . *recalc . . .* We're totally all over it. *Recalc . . .* I never fail." Again, your ultimate destination was never in jeopardy, the light got through the crack, a new way was found, and your arrival remains assured.

In Steamy, Sexy, Romantic Hookups

In real life, however, not only is there chaos in your own adventures, switching up possible manifestations that remain true to your roving focus, but the world has seven and a half billion other minds that are also changing, on the fly, and so the morphing, changing, and recalculated manifestations must keep flowing, in tune with all.

In fact, most of our big dreams even depend on other people! No problem, *as long as we're not talking "specific" other people,* such is the ability of Divine Mind to "recalc" on the fly. You might want more clients, for example, readers for your new book, customers for your new retailing adventures, lawyers for your new business dealings, and the like. Great! No problem! There are loads of candidates; Divine Intelligence will find those who complement your

dreams, and you theirs. There's always going to be a perfect someone when your end results are on the left side of the Matrix. If
later, the matched person changes their mind or priorities, *recalc*!
Instantaneously, Divine Intelligence knows someone else!

Bruno

Let's just say that in your life right now, what you'd really,
really, *really* like, is a travel partner . . . with benefits. HOT! Smokin'
hot, loves you like crazy, reads the same books, laughs at the same
jokes, somebody who gets you like you get them. These details
are exciting, right? Cool, that's the point, up goes your emotional
vibration. Go ahead, make your menu list, "Tall, bald, author . . ."
*As long as you're not attached to any of these details, such menu-list
items are adding rocket fuel for a swift and happy manifestation.*

Put this energy out in the world, and instantly the Universe
is jumping up and down like an eager schoolboy, "*I know who! I
know who! I know who!*" In the split second you achieved clarity of
intent, the Universe interviewed seven and a half billion players.
And of those screened, the perfect person for you is . . . Bruno. He
lives in Milan, Italy. Wow! Except that's a long way from Kansas,
Toto. It's just as well that you don't hear the Universe. Because you
don't have any plans to go to Milan. In fact, you won't get to know
who he is, or if he even exists, until you meet him. You don't get
any confirmation that things are going to work out. You just have
to go on faith (or better, understanding). *Talk about adventure.*

Bruno's out there, but you don't get a sneak peek, and after a
while, you may consciously forget your request. Maybe weeks will
go by, and nothing. Then, one afternoon, the phone in your cubi-
cle rings. It's . . . *Mary*! Who? "Mary!" The voice sounds so familiar. Mary from high school, the one you affectionately called "Mad
Mary"! She's tracked you down using Facebook! She was the one
poking you under a pseudonym! She now lives in Seattle (Phew!
Far away)! You're starting to blush as you remember the crazy trouble you two stirred up back in the day. And you're thinking, *Oh no,
oh God, I wish she had just minded her own business. She's the last*

person I ever wanted to see again. Yeah, she changed her name five times, but now she's back to Mary. Turns out she went into fashion, the couture shoe business to be precise. And she says, "Hey, we gotta get together! We had so much fun back in school! Let's do it all over again!" And Mad Mary adds that every fall she goes to *"Hotlanta, girl!"* for the Atlanta Apparel Market, where the world in fashion, couture, and textiles convenes annually. "Let's meet in Hotlanta!" And you're thinking to yourself, *There's no way I will ever be seen in public with Mad Mary again!* But you steal a glance at your calendar, even before she stops talking, and you hear yourself say out loud, "Hell to the Yes, girlfriend! Let's do this, honey!" Neither of you have changed one bit.

> There's always an infinite number of possibilities *until you attach to an unimportant detail—* and all details are unimportant.

Even though weeks have passed and you may even have forgotten your menu list for a travel partner, because you still want one and you're getting out more, the game is still on.

Meanwhile, an ocean away, Bruno's phone rings. It's his sister. In tears. The family is beside themselves with worry over his latest fling, Trixie. He's spending all of his time, energy, and money on this very unhappy young lady who seems never to be satisfied. "Why can't you see what everyone else sees, Bruno?" Now, might you guess, living in Milan, Italy, what industry Bruno's sister works in? Right! Couture! Fashion! Shoes! *What a coincidence!* Not.

Now, might you also guess where she goes every fall? Atlanta!

"Bruno, dear brother-I-love, Mom said she'll pay for your flight. We can go to Atlanta together! Just you and me, bonding, clearing out the cobwebs, gaining perspective! Will you go with me? Please?!" Bruno is so touched by this gesture and the outpouring of family love, he agrees.

The next thing you know, you're walking the red-carpeted aisles of the Atlanta Apparel Market, and the lights seem to suddenly dim and waiver. But no, actually, you're walking and texting again, oblivious to the huge, hulking beast of manhood you're about to

collide head-on with. Bruno, too, is texting. Trixie's not happy
. . . WHAM! A collision of two bodies in motion. Cell phones and
sunglasses go flying, you both land square on your butts, choco-
late falls into the peanut butter, dazed and confused, and then
. . . your eyes meet, lock, and nothing, for either of you, is ever
again the same.

*This is how you've been doing "it" your entire life, and it's how
you can do anything else you might ever dream of.* Countless little
coincidences, miracles, and serendipities are orchestrated by the
Divine through the crack of chaos, ordained by your thoughts
(end results, dreams), reaching you however they could best reach
you, so that you would physically experience that which you were
thinking of at the outset. It never fails, always works, until . . .
until you start attaching to items on your menu list!

When It Won't Work

With every quality you attach to or insist upon, like, "He must
be tall!" you eliminate billions of candidates from contention! "He
must be bald!" Billions more. "He must be an author!" Forget it!
But you know better, don't you? At least now you do. Phew! But . . .
what if Bruno doesn't read *Playing the Matrix* in time? What if on
the day of departure, he calls his sister, crying man-tears because
of his unshakable love for Trixie, besides, she set his passport on
fire? It would seem like curtains, except at this stage you don't
even know he exists. And you don't need to, because, *"RECALC
. . . his name is Stan!"* and you're going to meet him in Denver this
November on your way to the ski slopes!

RECALC! RECALC! RECALC! There's always a workaround,
alternative, equally happy way. There's always an infinite number
of possibilities *until* you attach to an unimportant detail—and all
details are unimportant.

Do you think, understanding all I just shared, you'll ever
attach to an unimportant detail again? I think not, which means
we've achieved the point of this chapter.

CHAOS IS THE REAL DEAL

To give the chaos theory even more credibility, some scientists believe that the 20th century, one filled with countless technological breakthroughs, will nevertheless be remembered for only three new theories:

1. The general theory of relativity

2. Quantum physics (or quantum mechanics)

3. Chaos theory

Chaos is literally how the magic reaches us, and I believe the day is not far off when either our children, or our children's children, will actually learn about the Miraculous Mechanics of Manifestation in school, where all manifestations come to pass through the crack of chaos that exists among the illusions of time and space.

A Note from the Universe

Here's the trickiest of tricks:

Should you ever be in need of a miracle (you know, hypothetically, just "what if"), think not of the miracle, not even a little, but instead of its intended result.

Tallyho,
The Universe

Do you understand this Note? In this case, the "intended result" is your desired "end result." That's what you insist on. Do not dictate to the Universe, "I need this miracle, that miracle, and the other miracle, so that I can have X, Y, and Z." And don't think to yourself, *I must do this, that, and the other.* You can't know any of these variables. They're not knowable. There's a better way than micromanagement. Know what you want, generally speaking, get excited about it by imagining the details, and keep showing up, doing things, being available, so that Divine Mind will have the leeway and latitude necessary to figure out which way, which miracles, and all other logistics.

GETTING INTO THE DETAILS

The second step of three for Playing the Matrix is as simple as the first step, and it allows you to bring many of your old manifesting tools, like vision boards and affirmations, into the process without having to learn any new tricks. The only thing that is perhaps new to you is the notion that you need to leave room for even better than the details you've imagined, which is impossible if you are insisting on the old. Which really shouldn't be too hard to refrain from doing once you realize your idea of awesome details, limited to your life's experiences, would always pale in comparison to what Divine Intelligence might have in store for you, based upon the direction you give it with your end results.

Understanding this at a cellular level is as simple as understanding these lessons from this chapter:

1. The details are visualized to get you excited about your end results, not to be your end results.

2. There's always more than one right answer, path, possibility, partner, or nuance. So, insist upon none *or you exclude all others.*

3. When you insist upon any detail, you exclude a virtually infinite number of *better* ones.

4. When details become end results, you're actually messing with the cursed hows.

5. Make your menu lists—tall, dark, and handsome, whatever—just don't attach to them.

To tease you a bit into really understanding this, realize: you *can't* be too much into the details. The details are awesome!! This whole chapter boils down to whether or not you're *insisting* upon certain ones. If you are, big problem. If not, big plus.

TRY THIS AT HOME

Here we'll convert the Matrix into our first Matrix-based exercise. Using this form, I'm going to show you how to perform *Step 2, Getting into the Details,* as if you were Playing the Matrix to manifest more wealth and abundance, see figure 4.1.

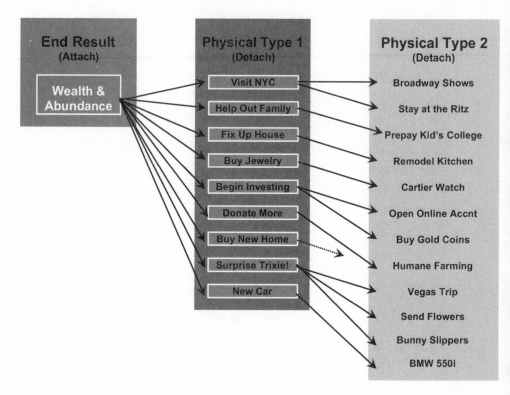

Figure 4.1

GETTING INTO THE DETAILS

The starting point is on the left, reflective of the ideal side of the Matrix to start from. In this example, we're starting with a Fantastic Five element, and then naming Type 1 details, followed by Type 2 details. By knowing what we want in general terms—Wealth and Abundance—we can then get into the details.

Here, we're dressing up the vagueness of Wealth and Abundance by filling up columns two and three on this chart with details *that excite us*; that make us passionately eager to create the change. Obviously, naming the left-most column enables the completion of the second, the second enables the completion of the third, also reflective of the left to right flow earlier shown in the Matrix, and, the flow of all manifestations in life.

Step 2 is where I said you'd get to put your own indelible mark on the process. While our desired generalities are often the same, how we each define these, in what capacities, colors, grades, priorities, etc., will vary.

To offer you a worksheet for this exercise that you might use as a guide for any similar type of form you can make up, it might look like the worksheet in Figure 4.2.

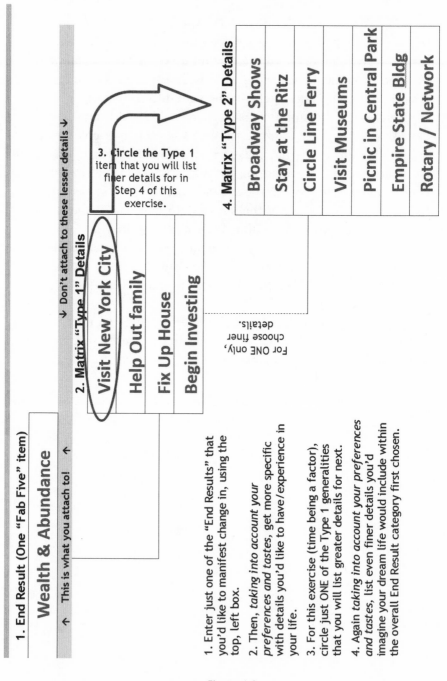

1. End Result (One "Fab Five" item)

Wealth & Abundance

← This is what you attach to!

← Don't attach to these lesser details ↓

2. Matrix "Type 1" Details

- Visit New York City
- Help Out family
- Fix Up House
- Begin Investing

3. Circle the Type 1 item that you will list finer details for in Step 4 of this exercise.

For ONE only, choose finer details.

4. Matrix "Type 2" Details

- Broadway Shows
- Stay at the Ritz
- Circle Line Ferry
- Visit Museums
- Picnic in Central Park
- Empire State Bldg
- Rotary / Network

1. Enter just one of the "End Results" that you'd like to manifest change in, using the top, left box.

2. Then, *taking into account your preferences and tastes,* get more specific with details you'd like to have/experience in your life.

3. For this exercise (time being a factor), circle just ONE of the Type 1 generalities that you will list greater details for next.

4. Again *taking into account your preferences and tastes,* list even finer details you'd imagine your dream life would include within the overall End Result category first chosen.

Figure 4.2

GETTING INTO THE DETAILS Worksheet

This table has been abbreviated simply due to lack of space. Using a journal or a computer document, you could certainly have more than four points in the middle column, and more than seven points in the third, for *every* detail you put in the second.

What you will find by completing and understanding this worksheet:

1. *This is not a to-do list.* That's in the next chapter. All you're doing now is getting immersed into details for the excitement they give you. Which is the entirety of Step 2.

2. Of the three columns on the worksheet, the one that is by far most valuable to you is the first one. You'd rather have abundance than just a picnic in Central Park, right? Or abundance over a new Ferrari. Right? And, quite clearly, the first column is by far the most general! Huh, imagine . . . Here we see that what is most important to us is the big, general, vague category, yet heretofore when we were excited about "manifesting" change, we rushed out to micromanage the unimportant!

3. Consider, if you used an adapted version of this form, and made your middle column 40 points long, and for each of those 40 details you created 40 more sub-details, you could then throw your reams of paper into a fireplace, start completely over with a different set of 40 details in the middle column, and a different 40 sub-details for each, *and these new details would be just as exciting to you as the first set.* Right? Showing how details are "a dime a dozen"! Easily replaceable. They're not important, in and of themselves. In this exercise, they simply represent the frosting on the cake of your dream come true. Again, they are not the cake!

Alternatively, a slightly different version of this exercise (one that I prefer):

1. Take a deck of five-by-seven-inch ruled index cards, and at the top of any number of cards you'll write down end results and priority areas in which you'd like to see transformation. Some cards may be very general, like "Happiness" or "Health," and on a few you might "dabble" on the right side of the Matrix, writing down "My New Car" or "My New House."

2. On each card, based upon its heading, you'll then jot down as many details as you can think of that get you excited about the imagined manifestation or transformation. In this version of the exercise, I don't even bother to differentiate between Type 1 and 2 details. With every jotted bullet point I get more excited! *Oh, yeah,* I'll think as I write, *I want my new home to have a tile roof! A fireplace! A well! A swimming pool! Lots of privacy! Convenient to work and nearby shopping!*

A Note from the Universe

I always knew I could count on you to uncover the truth. I wasn't surprised at all to find you standing by your principles when the going got tough. And there was never any doubt in my mind that when faced with a fork in the road, you'd take the path less traveled.

I just had no idea you'd have such expensive taste.

You so rock,
The Universe

P.S. Good thing we're rich, huh?

The Matrix has three objective steps. We've done the first two together in this book. Your homework for this step, in addition to the exercise just named, might be to create vision boards, affirmations, or to have visualization sessions in which you picture, imagine, and revisit these details, daily, to stay in the excitement of what your life will soon be looking like.

> It's so easy. *There is no advanced course!* "Thoughts becoming things," once truly understood, really is your black-belt Ph.D.!

Now, should you be thinking, as some audience members have volunteered, *Mike, I love it. Great job. I totally get it. But Mike, just wondering, do you have anything, you know, more advanced?* Ack! Please, let it be simple. Such questioners simply haven't yet been convinced that our mortal job in bringing about great life changes is the easy part. You need not know anything else. It doesn't matter who you used to be. Doesn't matter where you used to be. It doesn't matter that quantum physicists still have not yet discovered that one unifying equation that ties together all physical and metaphysical laws, because in the meantime, our thoughts will still become things, *which is all anyone ever has to know!* What matters is that you deeply understand the simple ground rules we're covering, and then start applying them from today forward. It's so easy. *There is no advanced course!* "Thoughts becoming things," once truly understood, really is your black-belt Ph.D.! The only other thing that might get in your way are the nuances, the Bermuda Triangle of Manifesting that we've been talking about, which the Matrix automatically navigates around.

You're going to be unstoppable . . . You already are.

Chapter 5

TAKING ACTION

Taking action simply means *showing up*, consistently. Moving in the direction of your dream, as best you can. It does *not* mean getting more spiritual—meditating, visualizing, creating affirmations, or becoming a vegan. It means taking baby steps, down unglamorous dirt paths if necessary, rather than waiting for "Easy Street" to magically appear beneath your feet—maybe it means doing what your friends and peers are doing, making cold calls, going back to school to brush up on skills, joining leads groups or dating websites, eating mindfully, pressing the flesh, networking, and the like.

> **Realize for every little step you take, you increase, exponentially, what the Universe can do for you.**

I'm often asked how one might take "massive action," again, as some schools of thought encourage, while simultaneously *never* messing with the cursed hows. "Isn't this an oxymoron? Doesn't doing one mean you are doing the other?" The same seeming paradox as getting into the details but not attaching to them.

THE CURSE TO AVOID

Understand, you will always be working various "hows" in your life, doing X to invite Y. Similarly, you will always be surrounded by details and there will always be specific people you engage with. None of which are problematic *until you start demanding, expecting, insisting, and attaching.* Right? And such stems from how we define our actions and how we choose to view why we do them.

Therefore, a "how" only becomes cursed not for what you do, but for how you view why you did it. Simply:

- If you are doing X to make your dreams come true, it's a cursed how.

- If you are doing X, *among other things*, to engage life's magic, create possibilities, and have fun, you're going to be a manifesting rock star.

Notice, X is the same in both scenarios. The only difference is your rationale for doing it. In the latter instance, through diversification alone:

1. you've reduced stress

2. you've created more possibilities for success

3. you are possibly navigating around unknown limiting beliefs,[2] and

4. you've left room for "even better" than you knew to ask for.

Add to these perks to "have fun in the pursuit" . . . and the process becomes win-win-win.

Two people could do the same thing, for instance. For one, it's a cursed how and they're carrying the weight of the world on their shoulders. And for the other, it's just a knock on the door, one of many, there's no attachment or insistence, "might work out, might not."

---

2   Did you catch that? That was *Limited-Belief-Busting Freebie Tip #2.*

A Note from the Universe

You don't take "baby steps" for the distance they cover, but to put yourself within reach of life's magic.

Just like you don't hoist your sails to move the boat, but to put yourself within reach of the wind.

Hoist, baby, hoist, baby, 1, 2, 3, 4—
The Universe

P.S. Just like you don't sing in the car to be heard . . .
Why do you do that?

As any skipper will tell you, the unfailing winds of the Universe will utterly escape you, until you hoist your sails (do your part) to put yourself within their reach. Position yourself; do what you can with what you have from where you are. You must show up, be there, do your part. *Only then can the Universe do its part.* The more you do, the more it does. You keep going. It keeps going. You stop. It stops.

Choose to see your baby steps as how you'll put yourself within reach of life's magic. Realize for every little step you take, you increase, exponentially, what the Universe can do for you. That with every single step you invite possibilities, multiply chances, and create probable worlds to love and be loved in that would not otherwise exist.

For the energy created and the anticipation aroused, doors start opening. Even doors you didn't knock on, but that wouldn't have opened had you not been busy.

MY BABY STEPS

I'm often asked what my baby steps were, so, with the intention of giving you some ideas and parallels, I'll return to my story from Chapter 3, when after praying to God on my knees, I knew to follow up those prayers with my often mentioned "moving feet."

The Least Sucky Paths

Scared for my life, wondering what brought on the "train wreck" and how I might move forward from it, I derived a sure-fire formula to give me direction, that anyone else can follow too, should they reach the bottom of their rope and have no tunnel to look for a light in:

Three Steps for Creating Direction When You Have NONE

1. Assess your sucky options.
2. Give yourself a deadline, maybe a couple of days.
3. Choose the *least* sucky of those options, and get busy.

Then, at least, you're under sail.

> It was a sucky path that promised nothing. Yet it was better than doing nothing.

This is not to imply, "Choose your least sucky paths and learn to love them." Hell no! This is just to get you out of the house! With your generally stated end results already prioritized, the Universe is pressing out all that you need for transformation. But until you leave the house, you're unreachable. And while you're at it, be sure *not* to choose just one path!

Remember, this is advice to readers who have nothing going on in their life and no idea of where to begin. Begin anywhere, and this is how. If you do have something going on, but dream of living larger while not knowing what to do next, then keep doing what you're doing, as you also begin knocking on new doors and trying new paths.

My Least Sucky Paths

I had a lot of sucky paths to consider, I guess we all do. But my *least* sucky paths were as follows:

1. *Go back into the corporate world.*

I polished off my old accountant's résumé, and added to it my decade as an entrepreneur, and quickly found that taking action breeds clarity. A clarity that could not have come in any other way than for the steps I was taking. The clarity that came to me while circulating my CPA résumé for eight weeks . . . was nausea. And I wasn't alone! To my total shock and amazement, turned out the hiring world was equally nauseous at the prospect of my return, evidenced by no one even offering me an interview! I had thought I was a rather hot ticket, given my impressive past. No. Turns out, living off of the corporate grid for a decade to run your own start-up, that eventually became a "mop-up," is not particularly impressive. Yet, knowledge is power, and for no longer deluding myself about my corporate marketability I was better able to double down on my efforts elsewhere, which had already begun in tandem with this first step.

2. *Dabble with creative writing.*

The World Wide Web was rather new in 1999, but for a couple of years prior to liquidation I was sending out an e-mail called a "Monday Morning Motivator" to those who'd signed our retail store guestbooks, not that they had asked for such. We had several thousand addresses, and every Monday, along with an inspirational poem I had written for one of our T-shirts (they were about life, dreams, and happiness, anyway), we'd offer them a "Deal of the Week"! Hardly anyone bought anything, but it was cool. Just the thought of reaching people scattered around the globe, with the press of a button, made my mind spin. Grateful to Al Gore for inventing this contraption, and possessing an eagle eye myself for trends (wink), I looked to the web for possible new directions. Just because we had ceased business operations, I didn't want to lose my e-mail connection with former customers, but how to keep it going?

What would be the point of future "Monday Morning Motivators" if there were no deal to offer, no product to sell? I racked my brain and the best I could come up with, staying in character of the company they would remember, would be to send out a weekly poem from an old T-shirt for its hoped-for motivational value, followed by a two- or three-paragraph essay on the deeper meaning of the poem.

I did *not* want to do this. The e-mails were unsolicited to begin with. Motivation of any kind can easily come across as arrogant. And worst of all, I was in no place at this stage of my journey to be telling other people how magical life was! It was a sucky path that promised nothing. Yet it was better than doing nothing. To move myself into this direction, and I highly recommend this whenever needed, I had to trick myself, consciously and with full knowledge, into the first essay: *Just do it one time, Mike. Just once. If you bomb or really regret it, you're off the hook. But if it goes well, maybe it'll pave the way for something better.*

I spent a full eight-hour day on the first Monday of the year 2000 writing an e-mail that extolled the virtues of creative visualization, and berated myself the whole time. I argued, *I'm sure Louise Hay, Dr. Deepak Chopra, or Dr. Wayne Dyer have already said this much better than I could ever hope to!* Yet taking action bred clarity. By the end of the day I had written that the reason we visualize is "because our thoughts actually create a mold that the elements of time and space can later rush to fill . . ." *Dang, Dooley, I bet Dyer never said it like that before!!!* I finally hit SEND, to some 2,000 e-mail addresses, and, perhaps, not intentionally and without malice, I became a spammer, probably among the first in the world. Although, to be fair to myself, no one ever heard from me who hadn't personally given me their e-mail address, understanding they eventually would.

More clarity quickly arrived. Unlike earlier mailings and their related "Deal of the Week," to which no one replied, this e-mail got fan mail and appreciation! Whoohoo!!! As more and more Mondays rolled on by, and more and more "Motivators" were sent, I started to receive praise, like, "Thanks for writing us, Mike! I'm looking forward to Mondays because of you!" and another that I still have to this day, "I hope you're saving these for a book one day, Mike. They're really good!"

The weeklies turned into dailies, and almost a year later, the first *Note from the Universe* emerged—*which never would have seen the light of day had I not taken this sucky path, but instead, waited around on my couch for a "really good idea"*! It never would have come, or, if it had, I never would have recognized its merit nor had an audience to test it out on.

Still, at the time and to this very day, the *Notes* were free, and this was by no means the life of my dreams. I still had a large mortgage, even larger fears, and no income.

3. *Become a webmaster.*

Naturally, as I felt an inner green light for those e-mails, a natural extension was to build a website supporting them. I did all the logical things, like host an About page, have a sign-up page, and then I created an Ask Mike forum. Of course, I had to ask Mike the first few questions. I dabbled with other pages and concepts. I tried selling products, experimented with viral marketing, became an affiliate of complementary websites, learned about programming and scripts, offered free e-cards, and even had an interactive community helping life adventurers to meet one another. Every single thing I did to make money over the next 15 months failed—and although I've been told a number of marriages came from the free community, I was probably its only member who remained dateless.

4. *Explore becoming a professional speaker.*

So, I thought, getting a little logical as I advocated earlier, *if you're finding that you like writing these e-mails on life, dreams, and happiness . . . and you've always been deeply passionate speaking about such with family and friends . . . then maybe you should create an avenue for financial abundance to reach you through professional speaking?* It's well known that a good professional speaker can get paid a lot of money for a keynote, easily $10,000, $20,000, even $30,000 for a 45-minute talk! But just the fleeting thought of me speaking to an audience *terrified* me.

a. **I joined Toastmasters.** Toastmasters (www
.toastmasters.org) is an organization with thousands
of clubs all over the world that gives its members
weekly speaking opportunities at every meeting
to help them get over the fear of giving speeches
in public. It's a safe place to develop oration and
presentation skills, other than an environment like
your office or among clients, where you may fall on
your face with grave consequences.

It was awful. For *weeks* prior to my "icebreaker," I
was nervous. I spent an entire Saturday and Sunday
writing it, word for word. So scared was I on speech
day that I read from my written script, standing in
front of my club. Bad idea. The papers could then
be seen and heard ruffling in my shaking hands.
My voice kept breaking. My mouth was dry. Knees
were knocking. And I seriously wondered if anyone
could see my heart beating because it was pounding
so hard (they couldn't, not possible if you're wearing
clothes). Then, the "Ah Counter" of the meeting, a
rotating, volunteer position charged with counting
everyone's "Um's," "Ah's," and similar stammers
while ringing a bell for every infraction, was off the
hook, "Ding! Ding! Ding! Ding! Ding! Ding!" I was
sure she was making them up (you don't usually
hear your own Um's and Ah's), I couldn't understand
her seeming insanity. Anger mounting, I abruptly
stopped to give her the evil eye, yet upon returning
to the script I found I'd lost my place, adding further
to embarrassment. As I eventually resumed speaking,
she resumed dinging. I stared at her again, and lost
my place a second time. All for a measly four-minute
talk, about myself, in front of 12 people!

The clarity I got, however, was that other than
pity me, the audience really couldn't care less about
my terror, I didn't faint or cease functioning in any
way, and, I could write a damn good speech. That

first speech, incidentally, began, "I can't tell you about myself unless I share the guiding principle that leads me every day, 'Thoughts become things . . .'" I proceeded to enter competitions, win trophies, and, mostly, give better speeches.

b. **I spoke at Rotary Clubs.** I've never shied away from asking for help, and having met the occasional visiting professional speaker, I'd inevitably ask, "How might *I* get started?" More than once, I was advised, "Go speak at Rotary Clubs. They won't pay you, but they meet weekly, all over the world, and every meeting includes a guest speaker from the community, which could be you."

You probably can't even imagine how uninspired Rotarians were with me at 7 o'clock in the morning talking about "thoughts become things," creating vision boards, and crafting positive affirmations. They were rude. They'd sometimes cut me off before my allotted time expired. Hurry me on out. The only revenge I could think of was to speak at more Rotary Clubs! I hit up about 12 of them over the year that followed. What else was I going do? *What else are you going to do?* You can't wait. It's not an option. Speaking at Rotary, among the other things I was busy with, felt right and made far more sense than my other sucky options. So I kept at it.

Finally, a Rotarian came up to me after my talk at the 12th club, and in deep gratitude she said, "Mike, you were speaking to me today. Thank you!" I replied under my breath, "About time." She continued, "You know, Mike . . . you've brought your message to the wrong audience?" "*Really?*" I could hardly keep a straight face. "You should speak at my Unity Church, I'm on the board, our minister is about to go on vacation . . ."

c. **I tried Unity.** At first I balked, "I don't do churches!" But at her insistence—"They would totally eat you and your message up, Mike"—I agreed. Only to find there'd be 300 people in attendance! I was a wreck. I had to *memorize* a 30-minute speech, for fear my nerves would cause me to go blank. Yet, despite my fears, something unforgettable happened that day.

Those Unity people laughed at my every joke. They laughed at my every *attempt* at humor. And they laughed at things that still make me wonder . . . Not just a little; they roared! Bellyache laughs. It was like a dream. They were so happy and grateful. The church was so festive. And at the end of the service, I swear it seemed that all 300 stood in a very long line waiting to thank me for being their guest speaker that Sunday. And that was the first time, about two years into my sad and flailing journey, that I thought to myself, *I could do this . . . I could so do this.*

Steps on My Sucky Paths

Now, well on my way down sucky paths, here are some of the steps along those paths that I either took or that overcame me:

1. *Asked for more help.*

I had asked for help earlier, as indicated, yet this time the outcome was so astonishing that this step is worth revisiting and highlighting.

Driving home from my "Rocky Balboa Unity talk," my spirits were dashed when it dawned on me, *Now, I don't just write for free, I speak for free!* And I couldn't help admitting that as happy as that audience made me, it was just a talk, and my life still seemed incredibly stuck. I had to do more. So, from experience, seeking the counsel of others, nine out of ten people will give you T.M.I.— *too much information!* One out of ten will be too busy, bless them. I asked Dr. Wayne Dyer for help. He was too busy. I also asked the president of the National Speakers Association, Central Florida Chapter, how I might launch a speaking career. "I'd love to help you. Let's grab a few beers!" We promptly spent two hours talking over a six-pack . . . but not about me becoming a speaker; instead the conversation veered to how he might make bigger bucks on the Internet using the viral marketing techniques I was then learning. I remember driving home not a whit wiser, and thinking to myself, *It's just as well because I hate speaking!*

Have you ever noticed how sometimes in life when you knock on one door, a different one opens that you didn't even know was there, that's a whole lot more attractive than the door you were knocking on, *and that wouldn't have opened had you not knocked on the door that never did open*? I have and it's become one of my favorite teaching points.

Four days after the fruitless beer night out with my speaker friend, he called *me* up: "Mike, you've got a database of 3,000 people and so do I. Why don't we do an inspirational, self-improvement audio program that we'll sell on the Internet to our respective databases. Another friend of mine, a professional speaker, has been teaching me everything we need to know about how to create it, position it, and sell it." I *could-not-believe* that the president of NSA Central Florida would call *me* to do a joint venture with *him*! What!? "Oh yes, baby!" I came up with a title for our project, "Infinite Possibilities: The Art of Living Your Dreams." And he was like, "Wow." In fact, I was like, "Wow." Thinking to myself, *I need to hear that for my life!* I hesitated on the landing page he wanted me to put on my site, which as he described, "would list all the benefits to be received by the listeners of our program" (I thought it was too salesy). But he politely reminded me of where my life was at the time. Besides, he said, we'd offer everyone a 100 percent money-back guarantee. "Okay, I'll do it."

The idea was, every month we'd each send our respective subscribers a one-hour recording about living the life of their dreams. People could either buy them one at a time, or pay in advance for all 12 installments at a substantial discount. So, I did everything he said, right down to the salesy landing page. We hadn't even recorded word one. We took it to our respective lists. And in the first night, I sold over $5,000 worth! Ah!!!!!!!!!!! I was happy-dancing like a fool. I called him with the news, he didn't believe me. He said he had sold "None!" I didn't believe him. I asked, "Did you list all the benefits to be received by the listener?" And he said, "No, I thought that was too salesy." I didn't know it then, but this was the light getting through the crack. I've come to notice that when you have weird, unpredictable, illogical things happening in your life, it's the light. It did not make sense.

> We don't usually know about most miracles until long after they happen. This is where faith, *through understanding,* comes in.

And then the best thing of all happened, although at the time it didn't seem like it. He backed out. "You don't have to split that money with me. Just do it yourself, and one day I'll do my own version of Infinite Possibilities." What? WHAT! I didn't know if I should be happy or mad. And I hardly had time to decide because I wasn't about to refund anyone's money and the first installment was due to my new subscribers in 10 days!

I asked, "How am I going record this audio program on my own?" He said, "Go buy a Sony Walkman MiniDisc player. Record it in your house." And then I wondered to myself, *How am I going to get paid?* before realizing that due to my earlier failed product sales, my online shopping cart was credit card enabled, which meant the $5,000 was *already in my bank account!* What would I record for the first hour installment? I cobbled together my Toastmaster speeches, about a dozen of them, forged segues, tweaked and edited, and BANG, it was done. "Thoughts Becoming Things!" was the title of the first hour.

How would I sell beyond my list? Which was the problem I had when offering other, earlier, flop products (like new T-shirts, "survival kits," and various trinkets). Those who bought them did so when first announced; after that, virtually nothing. My database was too small, and I had no other market. Well, by then, all the viral and affiliate marketing tricks I learned could be used to promote *Infinite Possibilities*. In fact, I started contacting people with big e-mail lists and they became *my* affiliates.

A Note from the Universe

The few who look forward, while always knocking on new doors, no matter how futile it may seem or how insignificant their progress, will carry the many who just keep waiting for things to get better.

And the few will "suddenly" become overnight legends within their families, 'hoods, and countries, while having the most fun, with the most friends, at the most after-parties.

Win/Win, baby—
The Universe

P.S. "While always knocking on new doors, no matter how futile it may seem or how insignificant their progress . . ."

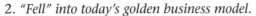

2. *"Fell" into today's golden business model.*

Any quick or deep study of ideal business models on the Internet today will reveal that in addition to having a database of e-mail addresses (a platform), you should have a free service (*Notes from the Universe*) coupled with optional purchases for those who want more (*Infinite Possibilities*)! *Et voilà!*

In addition to my guerilla affiliate marketing scheme, every day, almost, when I sent out the free *Note*, I would include a brief mention of *Infinite Possibilities* with a link for its purchase. So as not to overwhelm subscribers with this constant sales plug, on some days I made no mention of it, and on others, I would try to impress them by suggesting that if they happened to be in Miami (or wherever) in three Sundays, they could come hear me speak for free at whatever Unity Church I was to be speaking at next, on the topic of "Thoughts Become Things"! I realized that of my few thousand subscribers who were scattered around the world, maybe only three would be in driving distance of the church, but

I mentioned it nonetheless to my entire database thinking they'd be so impressed that I'm really out there talking about this stuff, they'd be more likely to buy *Infinite Possibilities* the next time I mentioned it in a *Note!*

Yet again, by knocking on one door, another opened that I could have never dreamed of. I don't really know how many people, if any, were inspired to buy my audio program with this "approach to impress," but because of my repeatedly telling my entire list I was speaking here, there, and anywhere I could get my foot in the door at a Unity Church, one day an e-mail arrived from, of all places, Holland. "Dear Mike, my wife and I love your *Notes* and we're duly impressed by the initial installments of *Infinite Possibilities.* Now we see that you're available as a speaker (evidenced by my frequently announced Unity Church gigs) . . . what would it take to have you speak at our quarterly Herbalife downline meeting?"

3. *How many cities constitute a world tour?*

What?! Are you kidding me? My first proper speaking gig might be in Europe?

a. **Amsterdam, Holland, by way of Orlando, Florida.**
   I didn't know "what it would take" to have me speak there! I called my speaker friend and he said, "Well, you're a total rookie, so not too much. On the other hand, international gigs command a premium. Tell them $5,000." Ak-k! That was about how much I would have paid to be able to say I spoke in Holland! I told them $5,000, and the next day they replied "You're hired." *Yes! Clutch! Wait a minute . . . No, no, no! I'm not ready!* I thought in great fear. I asked, "How many people are you expecting?" And they said, "Oh, about 110." Gasp! "And how long am I going to speak?" "Well, you're coming a long way, at least four hours." *Horror! Four hours! Who could possibly talk for four hours?! They're insane! But . . . it's $5,000 . . . !*

For a rookie speaker, you want nothing more than to be booked. But as soon as you are, you want nothing more than to cancel it!

I wondered how I could ever pull this off. I'd never spoken for longer than 30 minutes! After several panic attacks, I had a plan. "I'll do my first event in Orlando. It'll be my own event, scheduled two weeks prior to the Amsterdam event. Announce it to my list, alone. Three people will be in driving distance. It'll be a safe audience, not too much risk, and it'll give me a trial run before flying to Europe." So, I told *Notes* subscribers, "Hey, come hear me speak at my first-ever workshop, open to the public, 10 to 3 o'clock, $95 and I'll buy you lunch!" To my great chagrin, people started signing up from all over the U.S. This was terrible. About 40 people in all, 37 too many.

I remember stirring my coffee at the little stand inside the Hilton Orlando Lake Buena Vista, and two ladies came rushing up to me, "Are you Mike? You're Mike Dooley! Oh God! *We're so excited!* Last night we flew in from San Francisco! *Whoohoo!*" "San Francisco?" I replied incredulously . . . "_Why did you do that?!_" The pressure to perform was palpable. I hated it. I hated life. I hated myself. I hated everything. I was visibly shaken during the entire event, but taking action breeds clarity. To my surprise, and I should have known better, they didn't care that I was nervous. *I had something to say.* I could write a darn good presentation. Everyone, including me, left the event happy! It was a day I will never forget.

I went to Amsterdam, same thing!

b. **London, England.** No sooner had I returned home, still on Cloud 9, another e-mail was waiting. "Dear Mike, I'm writing from London, England. A big fan of yours. What would it take to have you come speak in the U.K.?" "$5,000!?"

"You're hired!" And then he added, "Let's sell it to the public." He said, "I'll tell my peeps and you tell yours, it'll be a joint venture for which we share the proceeds." Wow! But my speaker friend warned me, "Make sure he pays you a deposit 30 days out! Speakers get burned every day!" He agreed. Meanwhile, I'm selling seats to my subscribers and had bought my own plane ticket, yet 30 days out, he didn't pay the deposit.

Two weeks out he still hadn't paid, and he wasn't returning my phone calls! I finally got a call from his assistant to find they had a falling out over money, and the event was canceled. "What?! Why wasn't I told earlier?! Does the hotel know?" No, the hotel didn't know. I called the hotel, "Don't hate the messenger . . . by the way, what were the terms? Will you renegotiate? I can carry this event if they're favorable." We did a brand-new deal. I went to London as planned. There were about 40 people, again. I was a wreck. All loved the day. It turned a profit.

c. **The World.** I got home, and it stopped. Weeks turned into months turned into many months. I thought out loud, looking up as if to God, "What's going on here? You let me taste that, and then pull the rug out from under me? Is this some sick sense of humor?" Just when I thought I was found, I was lost all over again. Remember, I was still desperate, in debt, and afraid for my life. Sure, I had a few great trips, but a few great trips and about $15,000 does not translate into the life of anyone's dreams!

And then, a light went on in my head: I did Orlando myself. I did London myself. Nobody cares who's your sponsor, or even if there is one. Just look at your database of *Notes* subscribers and see where most of them live. Silently "invite" yourself, book hotel space, and . . . call it . . . *a World Tour!* After those first 3 events, 21 more followed over 18 months, including stops in Canada, Australia, New Zealand, Hawaii, and back to Europe, thanks entirely to *Notes from the Universe* subscribers.

Clearly, I was then under full steam, yet realize that at no time in a journey from lack to plenty is success on a specific path inevitable or assured, and no one knows this more than the one in the middle of the journey. Every event in that first world tour had my stomach in knots, I kept feeling I'd been "lucky" so far, and undoubtedly in the next one, I'd be going down. Self-doubt, insecurities, and my home mortgage haunted me every step of the way. Never did I wake up on a morning feeling like, *I made it! I'm living my dreams!* Yet still, only in hindsight, I had and I was. I mention this for two reasons: 1) Self-doubts and fear are normal in any journey, and they alone should not be allowed to stop you! Don't worry that you worry. As long as you continue doing all you can, with all you have, from where you are, you will become unstoppable. 2) I still had the rest of my life to figure out, as you probably do right now, which meant one thing, I and you, must keep on keeping on, no matter where we are.

4. *Shared a great secret.*

Returning from Europe, by then on my second self-proclaimed world tour, I received an e-mail from two sisters: "Dear Mike, we love your *Notes* and we have *Infinite Possibilities* on our iPods. We're in the TV/film business, writing you from Melbourne, Australia. We're coming to the U.S. to do a documentary on the law of attraction. Can we interview you?" That's how I got in *The Secret*. I don't know on what sucky, crappy day in my life they found me. Around that time, it was quite possibly one in which I drove by my mother's home after another Rotary Club bomb to bum a cigarette and tell her, "I hate speaking, when's my life going to take off?!" Yet somewhere in that time frame, Rhonda and Glenda signed up for *Notes from the Universe*. A big miracle day for me that I was completely unaware of. Remember, however, that just because you can't see the miracles doesn't mean they're not happening. They are. Every day. In *your* life. Today, even. KNOW THIS! We don't usually know about most miracles until long after they happen. This is where faith, *through understanding,* comes in. This is life's greatest hook—requiring us to behave in line with our dreams, not with what our physical senses are showing.

5. *Sold a book.*

When you're in something like *The Secret* that just blew up the world over, all the publishers who had earlier rejected your submissions, like mine for *Infinite Possibilities*, start calling *YOU*! I had a field day, the pick of the crop, took my time, and finally accepted a very handsome six-figure advance from Simon & Schuster (Atria and Beyond Words). And again, thanks entirely to *Notes from the Universe* subscribers, it debuted at number seven on the *New York Times* bestseller list.

> The train of my life never crashed. It just came to an abrupt standstill, *so that it could change tracks, upon which it could go farther, faster, higher, and better!*

When you have a *New York Times* bestseller, foreign publishers want it. They don't care about you. They don't even care about what you wrote. They want it. Today, my books are sold in 25 languages.

6. *Tried love.*

And when I least expected it, had begun thinking my chance had passed, I was invited to headline a four-day inspirational event with none other than don Miguel Ruiz, famed author of *The Four Agreements,* in Puerto Vallarta, Mexico. Whereupon I met a ravishing Mexican beauty, who spoke not a word of English, nor did I speak a word of Spanish (the Spanish-speaking audience wore headsets to hear simultaneous translation of my segments). To spare you a long and winding story filled with subsequent rendezvous around the world, we got married in spite of ourselves, and have since drawn the conclusion that not speaking your partner's language makes for a solid gold foundation in love. Today, nine years later, now doing well-enough in the other's language, we're still in love, and proud first-time parents to a daughter who bursts our hearts with joy, every single day.

I often fall to wonder, as you will one day if not already, whatever did I do in my human, flailing, mortal, desperate, badmouthing life to deserve so much. To even ask that question, of course, reveals that some of my "old wiring" (limiting beliefs) are still evident in my thoughts, but now, so is the truth—*we were all born deserving*. Even our own fears and negativity can't stop us when we learn who we really are and all we're capable of doing.

I can see so clearly today that even though for two years everything I did to resurrect my life seemed to fail, each such failure was actually a carefully orchestrated step toward all that I would later achieve. As if those nights at my bedside, when I said, "Dear God, I want abundance, friends, fulfilling work, and international travel," she replied, "*I know how! I know how! I know how! First, we need you to create some content, build a website, learn viral and affiliate marketing, get over your fear of public speaking, get credit card enabled, and find a peer who will raise your sites. Understand, however, you're not going see a single miracle the whole journey, until the end. Oh, and it's way too early for you to even be thinking about a vasectomy . . .*" But of course, we aren't privy to such replies. Faith—not a lot, it takes so little.

A Note from the Universe

Within any clearly imagined dream, far beyond the curtains of time and space, lies the intelligence and energy to choreograph the entire sequence of events necessary to make it manifest as soon as possible.

And if you physically move toward that dream, demonstrating both faith and belief, making yourself available to "accidents and coincidences," not insisting on the hows, and rolling with what may come, the sequence is permitted to play itself out.

Understand, however, that since you will only perceive this sequence with your physical senses upon a linear timeline, it will likely seem that much of your journey doesn't make sense, is unpredictable, or may even appear off-course.

Yeah, you're crushing it right about now—
The Universe

P.S. And here, right now, in the bleachers,
your name is being sung in a rising chorus
along with "We-e-e-e-e are the champions . . ."

TRAIN WRECKS ARE IN THE EYE OF THE BEHOLDER

One of the more common questions I receive from people is, "Mike, how do you handle setbacks? Like, when your life is going great, you're doing all the right things, and then, *SLAM*, you're blindsided by the unexpected. How do we know if this was our thinking or random, will it happen again, what conclusions can we draw, and how can we prevent this in the future?"

First, whenever the unexpected or unthought-of happens, it is *always* because just beyond it there was something you were thinking about, and the only way to get there was through the unthought-of territory. Thinking otherwise you jettison your power. You had control of whatever happened to you, albeit the reasons, purpose, and meaning behind such events is not always clear. But this neither means you must figure out why or how you specifically brought it about, nor does it mean it can or will repeat in the future. Best to simply claim responsibility for it, thereby retaining your power, and look ahead.

Second, I've used the term *train wreck* throughout this book because it's one we can all relate to, yet, while it indeed implies disaster, as you come to understand these things, you'll start seeing them as flash points more symbolic of hope than doom. In truth, as I trust I've also made clear, all setbacks are setups for greatness; self-arranged gifts, sometimes wrought of "chaos," that can take us higher than we could have gone without them. Always.

In my case, from the depths of my despair 17 years ago, I knew I didn't want to "look for what was wrong with me," nor try to explain, metaphysically, what had just happened, because if I had, I would've either found stuff or made it up. Instead of staring at the carnage of my train wreck, I doubled down on what I did know, how life, generally speaking, does work, that we are inclined to succeed, that our thoughts become things and we are born of, by, and for the Divine with default settings aimed at soaring.

Years later, however, when things in my life began rocking again, curiosity drove me to take a gander back at the earlier mess I had traversed, and to my utter shock, I could find no train wreck. As I had lamented, my life at 39 years old had no momentum. I had to start everything over again, as if from scratch. Prior to the mess, I wrote about life, dreams, and happiness for T-shirt ornamentation, and deeply longed that my words could reach more people than could be found shopping for novelty souvenirs in tourist destinations. After the mess . . . whoa, I could then see I still wrote about life, dreams, and happiness, through best-selling books, world tours, Internet courses, and more—exactly what I had been dreaming of.

> You're always going to be stirring the pot of possibilities with logic and intuition, and thereby giving the Universe more dots to connect on your behalf.

The train of my life never crashed. It just came to an abrupt standstill, *so that it could change tracks, upon which it could go farther, faster, higher, and better!* None of which was apparent to my worrying mind or physical senses! To the contrary, at the time of the commotion, all I could see was "bad stuff," my life in ruins, manifestations I had *not* thought about, and I was mightily at risk of assuming I was broken, bad, and irredeemable.

To those who ask me these days, "How do you handle bad stuff and setbacks?" I tell them there are no such things, they just need to give themselves time to see this. Meanwhile, I urge them not to draw negative conclusions, look ahead, stay in action, and reassure them that one day, this will all make perfectly good sense.

TAKING ACTION

Life is so *not* fair. The cards are stacked in your favor! Just make your end results general, get excited about them to the best of your ability, show up, do stuff, never stop. It's going to feel beneath you. It's going to seem futile, like my icebreaker speech at Toastmasters. But the physical senses deceive. They're the biggest liars in your life. You're a magic instigator! A manifesting matador! A natural born creator! Again, your positive thoughts are far more powerful than your negative thoughts. So, if you worry, or even have daily pity parties, ha! Enjoy them too, just be sure to do all else contained in this book, so that nothing can ever keep you down. In particular, for this chapter, understand:

1. Taking action summons resources, emboldens beliefs, and avails you of life's magic.

2. For every step you take, the Universe takes 10,000.

3. Sometimes knocking on one door forces another to open.

4. What you do is not as important as that you do it.

5. By trying many paths, you automatically navigate around invisible limiting beliefs.

6. Never stop asking for help, trying new directions, responding to conditions, innovating, evolving—stay in motion.

7. The more you enjoy and can afford what you do, the more specific you can be.

As promised in Chapter 3, here I want to speak on diversification for readers who already know where their passion lies (who know what they want to be when they grow up). If you both enjoy what you do and can afford to do it, then you can be more and more specific with your end results. I wouldn't tell Roger Federer, tennis legend, that he should also take up ping-pong and bowling "just in case." If you're that far along in your bliss and can afford to do whatever you're doing, keep on it! I'd tell Roger to go to the red column and visualize Novak Djokovic weeping on center court at Wimbledon because you've just beaten his pants off in the finals! Similarly, I'd tell anyone in their bliss, living within their means, that it's okay to go further into the blue and yellow columns with heightened determination, adamant and demanding of their further success. Sure, it might not work out for reasons beyond their control (given they're in the Bermuda Triangle of Manifesting), but since they have found what they love, this love, alone, will be adequate consolation as they continue onward toward new conquests after any such disappointments.

However, if either of these conditions are not met, diversify. And choose not to see diversification as settling for less; this is not creating a backup plan. Consider Mariah Carey, who has as many number one hits as the Beatles, minus two, was a waitress at a diner in Manhattan while she launched her singing career. Elvis Presley was a mechanic. J.K. Rowling, a struggling single mom. As I've already shared, you don't have to go forth in some blaze of glory, burn your bridges, do one thing, and never give up! That's for soap operas. You're a divine gladiator of love and joy. The Universe and life's magic

*offer immense leeway and wiggle room. You don't have
to be perfect, any slack will be picked up for you. You just
want to do your best, while living responsibly, covering
your bases, and paying your bills. You don't need the
pressure of "staking your claim and seeing it through come
hell or high water." Ugh! Yuck! No fun!*

8. Always consider your unique strengths, likes,
    and preferences when formulating each pathway
    you'll try out.

A Note from the Universe

Brilliant, civilization-changing ideas are a dime a dozen. Physically taking action to implement them, however, beginning with baby steps that seem to accomplish very little, is what gets the crowds here screaming like raving lunatics.

In the good way that lunatics scream . . . you know?

Peanuts! Popcorn! Cotton candy!
The Universe

Life is such a precious, fleeting gift. When it comes to formulating the action steps you'll be taking, consider those things that long ago thrilled you, because chances are they still do.

TRY THIS AT HOME

This time we're going to convert the Matrix into our second Matrix-based exercise. The hypothetical starting point here is creative, fulfilling work, *aka Livelihood*, in the Fantastic Five, see figure 5.1.

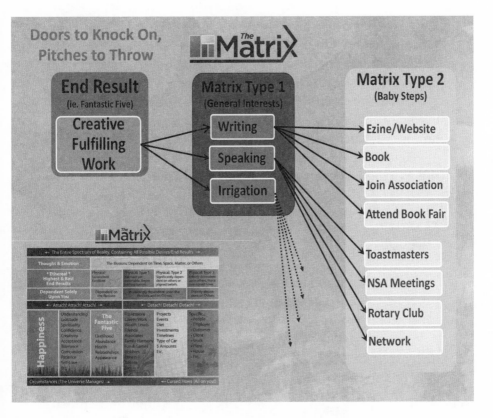

Figure 5.1

TAKING ACTION Diagram

While the flow looks exactly like Figure 4.1, the intention here is very different. Here the aim is to come up with action steps, physical "to-dos." In 4.1 it was simply to flesh out details that helped incite passion and excitement.

Similar to 4.1, our starting point is on the left, reflective of our ideal starting point in Playing the Matrix. Then, in the second column, we're naming General Interest areas that are *probably relevant to our starting point*, though if you are at a loss with the relevance angle, any interest areas will do. Once column two is done, then for each item in it we'll come up with concrete, specific things to do in the days, weeks, and months ahead.

Now we're leaping from the vagueness of Livelihood (Creative Work) to associate our interests with it, and then, to spur real action. Naming the left-most column enables the completion of the second, the second enables the completion of the third.

This step is another in which you get to put your own indelible mark on the process. Everyone wants a rocking livelihood, but how we each define and approach it will vary radically.

Figure 5.2 also looks identical to Figure 4.2. Like before, use this as a model for what you can create for yourself.

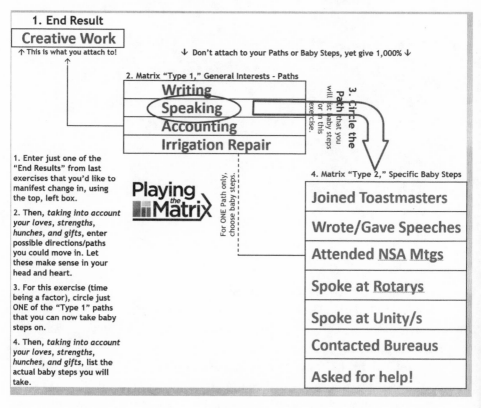

Figure 5.2

TAKING ACTION Worksheet

This reflects my story: writing, speaking, accounting . . . I spared you my love of irrigation repair, which never did get any action. Once you enter interest areas for direction, what remains are the concrete baby steps that you might now take.

I'd like to again point out the obvious. You could have more than four general interest areas. The more areas you have the more things there are to do and the quicker the Universe can reach you. *From each* interest area (not just one, like I've done in Figure 5.2 due to limited space), you will of course derive action steps, and you are most certainly not limited to seven. In fact, back in the day, I'd make new lists at the beginning of every week to ensure myself I'd stay busy. To this day, I'm constantly asking what else I could do to grow my business and life. Which has given birth to video programs, online courses, training events, interview series, kids' books, and much more. You're always going to be stirring the pot of possibilities with logic and intuition, and thereby giving the Universe more dots to connect on your behalf.

Alternatively, you can try a different version of this exercise, like in the last chapter:

1. Take a deck of five-by-seven-inch ruled index cards, and at the top of any number of cards write down one area of your life you'd like to see transformed. Some cards may be very general, like "Happiness" or "Health," and on a few you might "dabble" on the right side of the Matrix, writing down "My New Car" or "My New House."

2. On each card, based upon its heading, you will then jot down all the things, even seemingly futile, that you could now *physically* do that might "inch" you closer to the manifestation.

3. Later, of course, do them—like this week!

A Caution on Happiness as an End Result

While happiness is the ultimate end result, I'd like to point out something easy to forget.

I wouldn't want any reader, perhaps a year after reading this book, during a lull, to think, *Oh, I'm so frustrated that everything's taking so long . . . What did Mike say about happiness as the ultimate end result? That the Universe will take care of all the details and fire all the cylinders if we just insist upon happiness? Let me stop micromanaging and think only of happiness!*

YIKES! That would be an awful memory, because fully one-third of the steps listed to Play the Matrix is missing from recollection! *Even if your end result is the ethereal, nontangible quality of more happiness, you must take physical action toward it on a regular basis.* If you want any kind of change in time and space, you have to physically move. Now remember, your part is the easy part. You just show up. Hoist the sails. The Universe does the heavy lifting. But always, movement must be present, you taking action. As I said earlier, too often in my travels and talks with others, I see inaction. And waiting. And waiting. And waiting. Waiting for the magic; waiting for the Universe, who loves and adores those on the sidelines. *But you are unreachable on the sidelines.* You did not choose this life to be on the sidelines. You chose it to be on the field, engaged, playing, working, learning, reaching, stretching, and growing, even if on sucky dirt paths. You are an adventurer, above all.

I filled in the following hypothetical worksheet to show what I mean:

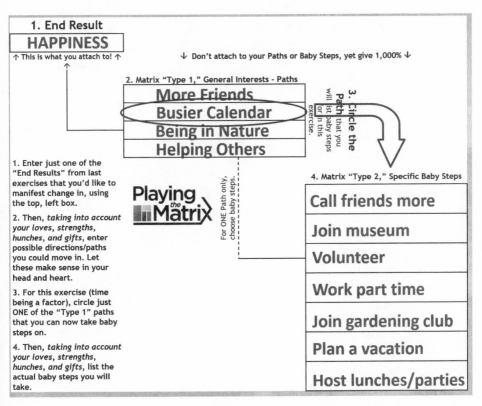

Figure 5.3

TAKING ACTION Worksheet 2

A Note from the Universe

Great big, ear-to-ear, open-mouth smiles are responsible for far more sizzling romances, salary increases, life extensions, and calorie burning than your dentists, doctors, and financial planners will ever comprehend.

Show us your tonsils,
The Universe

Fellow adventurers, we just outlined, and have a tiny bit of homework, for all three of the steps of Playing the Matrix. Stick with it even though at times you may seem to progress slowly, and the day will come when your view has irrevocably changed, and in almost disbelief, you'll exclaim, "Wow, that was fast!" And your life will be so sweet that you'll think to yourself, *I'd have waited 10 times longer, given how great it all worked out and how awesome everything now is.*

Chapter 6

EXPEDITED DELIVERY

With the tenets of the Matrix under our belts, all hinging on the simple, immoveable fact that our focus creates our reality, there's still more we can do to prime the pump of transformation.

The ideas here might actually fall under Step 2 of Playing the Matrix, *Getting into the Details*, not that we need to objectively place and identify what we're up to with labels and categories. All the tips and exercises to be reviewed are just fun things to do that powerfully add to, or build up, beliefs concerning our likely successes, no matter what our other, even limiting, beliefs may be *(Limited-Belief-Busting Freebie Tip #3)*.

Here we'll talk about using our thoughts, words, and deeds in playful ways, to create a heightened sense of anticipation, expectation, and optimism that will fuel the miraculous mechanics of manifestation like high winds feed a fire.

A Note from the Universe

There are indeed times in every life when one must simply lay low, hide out, and just chill.

And usually it's called sleep.

However, in between such times, by the light of the sun or a giant disco ball, I generally advocate as full a schedule as you can possibly manage.

Do the hustle,
The Universe

P.S. Besides, it's easier to fall in love,
and to be fallen in love with, when you're busy.

Doesn't the person who always has something to do and somewhere to go catch your eye? Their motion creates an air of purpose, fulfillment, and happiness. Any of us can be that person. Not only will it foster quicker manifestations, because you're out doing more, presumably happier (or about to become so) for your busy life, but just for the math of it, you'll make possible more opportunities for life's magic to find you.

YOUR THOUGHTS

In a word, visualize. It's the least you can do to get the most; the smallest effort you can exert for the biggest payout in life. Of course, as always, thinking but not acting isn't enough. Not because there's something other than thought in bringing about change. But if we're not acting on our thoughts, it's because there are other, conflicting thoughts. Thinking big but acting small is the same as thinking small. Want to know if your thoughts are in congruence with a dream? They are if you're physically doing something about them on a very regular basis.

Guidelines (not rules or laws) for Creative Visualization

1. *One time a day is all that's necessary.*
   You don't need to do it anymore. With one serious shot, you've created enough of an impression to convey the dream to the Universe. Let it go. Get back to the present moment. I take weekends off, you can too. Again, such is the leniency of life's magic.

2. No longer than 5 or 10 minutes at a time.

If you try to visualize longer, you'll invariably begin day-dreaming and then getting angry with yourself for losing your focus. Then you might even start labeling yourself adult ADHD, and begin believing you can't visualize! You can. It's easy. Give it just a few minutes each day.

To help with this one, you can use a timer. I used a kitchen egg timer for many years, until I thought to use my smartphone to silently count down four minutes, at which point an alarm sounds, and I'm done until the next day.

3. Ritualize it.

Make a daily routine out of it, like you do for brushing your teeth. In advance, choose the following: the time of day, the specific room in the house, a chair in that room, draw the blinds, and start the timer. You'll be far more likely to stick with a ritualized session than trying to remember "when you think of it and can spare the time."

4. Imagine every conceivable detail.

Sights, sounds, colors, textures, aromas. Make it as vivid as possible in your mind. The more details you conjure the more *believable* it will be, and the more believable, the more emotion you'll feel, and the more emotion, the faster the manifestation. Speaking of emotion . . .

5. Feel it.

Throughout each session, get into a space of joy. Fake it if you have to, and you probably will. You don't even have to have a reason for your joy, and not having a reason actually gives the Universe more leeway in bringing it to you later. Cut to the chase and imagine hearing congratulations from friends and strangers, smile ear to ear, clutch your fists, wave your palms, happy dance if you want (physically and/or mentally). Remember, it's joy and happiness that you're ultimately after, life's ultimate end result, and when followed up with action each day, all of life's details, players, and circumstances will be aligned and positioned so that you will authentically, materially be given cause to feel such joy all over again. This is how emotions become things, in part, by rearranging your *material* world!

6. *Script it in advance.*

Just a minute or so before you begin, decide upon a scenario you'll imagine moving through. Decide where you'll be, who with, doing what, when, where, why, etc. For example, you might be pushing a grocery cart through a familiar parking lot looking for your gorgeous new car. After you load it with your grocery bags, you're off to your new office space to see if the package from your publisher arrived. Yes! Your new book translated into Swahili was delivered at 9:49 A.M., you show it off to your co-workers before leaving for the local high school, where you will give a talk on entrepreneurship. By scripting it in advance you may be less likely to daydream and feel more engaged.

> Thinking big but acting small is the same as thinking small.

7. *Put yourself in the picture.*

Imagine yourself inside each image, experiencing all the details you're visualizing, seen from your eyes, heard from your ears, felt in your heart. This is your life, this is right now, this is happening to you! Let it be your hands on the steering wheel of your dreamed-of car. Your palm in someone else's palm as you walk side by side down the beach. Your toes in the sand.

8. *Dwell from the end result or beyond.*

Do not visualize your dream coming true. Right? See the twist? Again, do not visualize your dream *coming* true. Visualize your life as it will be *after your dream came true—past tense.* It's already done! You're already celebrating. Everything is super amazing, better than you had earlier imagined it would be. Now what are your dreams, your priorities, your challenges? This perspective implies you hit a total home run. That everything worked out. That you did it (not that you are doing it). Why? If you are "doing it," that would mean you are visualizing a "how," right? Imagine your life a week, a month, or a year after the dream has come true. Then, the only way this perspective could ever come to pass is if the dream has come to pass, and so it shall, with the freedom you left to Divine Intelligence to find the shortest, fastest, most harmonious way, maybe even in ways you hadn't thought of. Now the Universe will be unfettered by any imposed "hows" you would have visualized.

9. *Get physical when visualizing.*

I've learned these strategies by doing them. This last suggestion came about when I noticed I add a step to these guidelines when I visualize for one minute (using my timer) as part of my daily writing routine. In this exercise, I imagine (remember) what it feels like to have written a really good *Note from the Universe*—the emotion! *Whoohoo! I did it! It's awesome. I can't wait to send it out!* That's the end result I'm after every time I write, a feeling of euphoria for having written well. Of course, I haven't written anything yet, but the visualization is, It's done! I did it. I love it!

I do not visualize myself, for example, imagining that *today I will write about gratitude,* or whatever. Yuck! I would be constrained, limited, pressured, and the outcome would undoubtedly suck. I don't give any thought to "how" (as opposed to "what") I will write. What's different, however, from all the earlier guidelines, is that I notice that during this one minute I'd be pumping my fists, waving my palms, physically and audibly celebrating that I just wrote a great *Note*. And then, as soon as I'm done with this drill, which was step one of the Miraculous Mechanics of Manifestation, I do step two: Start writing, even though *I have no idea of what I will write.* Anything that comes to my mind. It's usually pretty bad. Invariably it gets deleted pretty quickly, but then I'm on to something else. I edit it. Cut and paste, delete some, add some, and within an hour or three, sometimes more, I get to that whoohoo place, the manifestation I was after, that was ordained by my earlier thoughts and theatrics.

Do you see, the only way I could ever get to my *felt* end result of "joy for having written well," *is if I write well!* The means, the hows are forced, emerging as I actually wrote, anything at first, to enable some "light to get through the crack." This is a mini-model of how to bring about *anything* your heart desires: Feel the desired celebratory emotion in advance, consistently do something about it, prepare to be astounded!

A Note from the Universe

There is only one explanation for your existence in time and space:

You wanted it so greatly, you imagined it so vividly, and you prepared for it so thoroughly you could literally taste it.

Get the picture?

This is also how to change your time and space, have more laughs, find more friends, and rock a gorgeous, new waterfront home . . . if you want one.

Tallyho,
The Universe

When you visualize with emotion, you create and send a very real energy from within that transcends and goes beyond the curtains of time and space, beyond where eyes can see. And there it whirls and twirls and collects and gathers. Then, *by law,* it comes silently sweeping back into your life as a bright idea, intuition, a new best friend, courage, confidence, clarity, pain-free living, whatever your heart desires, so that you can authentically have another one of those whoohoo feelings made manifest. This is how your thoughts become things.

YOUR WORDS

Choose your words wisely; they are your thoughts that will become things the soonest.

A friend of mine unintentionally reminded me again of how we (or, at least, I) can take so much for granted, and that such follies are easily found in the words we choose. Because all of our words, are chosen.

She and I would occasionally catch up over Skype, me in the U.S., her in Australia. The conversational tones were predictable. I'd speak in more of a monotone, "I went here . . . I had to go there . . . I was at the office . . . I had to write a few new *Notes* . . . I have a trip around the corner . . ." whereas she would hit every emotional tone on the scale, mostly the high ones. Excitedly

> **Speak good things! It doesn't matter that they might not be true today! This is how you make them true. This is how you got where you now are.**

telling me, "I went to Sydney last week!" "A client said I changed her life!" "I saw a rainbow!" "A dolphin followed me as I walked along the beach!" "You'll never guess who visited us last night? *THE TOOTH FAIRY!*"

In one of our conversations she blurted out, "Well, I'm su-u-u-re *something* good is happening in your life . . ." Wow. Ouch. "Yeah . . . it's a-l-l good!" You know, I rock. "Well, you never tell me about it," she added.

It took a moment to process, but, yow, she was right. Not about what I shared, but how I shared it. Unlike her, I shared everything without emotion, without celebration, and most notably, as if I were burdened with having to endure my life. My statements all sounded like, "I *have* to go here, I *have* to write a *Note*, I *have* to visit New York." I really thought I rocked, but I was misinformed. No way, we don't *have* to do jack, *we get to*.

Every day is a gift, the fleeting privilege earlier referenced. Nothing is expected, everything is given. And should we dare, we can leap, dream, soar, and live responsibly for the glories it will add to tomorrow, *if* we even get one more day.

Ever since that time, I've made it a point to listen to my own conversations, to clue into my appreciation or lack thereof, because when we're appreciating and celebrating what we *get to* do, it expands, we see more of it, we create more of it, have more fun, and an upward spiral lifts off. Simply from choosing our words wisely, which reflect the thoughts that are then the mightiest in our minds.

From this day forward, you can do the same. Simply pay attention to your own words. If you hear something that doesn't serve you, stop saying it, because to say it or to even repeat it day in and day out, you start creating and/or perpetuating it. Your friend, for example, who says he can't lose weight *is always right*. The Universe silently replies, *"Got it. Don't worry, you'll be in the wrong place at the wrong time with the wrong friends, predisposed to the wrong foods, no willpower, slow metabolism! Roger! Gotcha!"*

Your friend who says, "I love my life, love my wife, have all I want, except . . . I just can't crack the money nut," *will never crack the money nut!* The Universe is taking notes! Your words, like these, give lip service to your otherwise concealed end results, even if you don't think of them as end results, and even if you don't want them to manifest. This is how it works. You are a nonstop streaming manifestor! Based on what you choose to say, you will come across the most bizarre, unforeseen circumstances, making it possible to meet what you've been speaking. So speak good things! It doesn't matter that they might not be true today! This is how you make them true. This is how you got where you now are.

Start saying things you want to be true *as if they were true*. Speak of yourself as if you were already the person of your wildest dreams. Speak of your life as if you were already living as large as you now imagine. These statements are known as mantras or affirmations. You might choose to say: "I love my life. My life is easy. I have total clarity. I always say the right thing to the right person at the right time. I'm always in the right place at the right time. I'm surrounded by abundance. Everything I touch turns to gold. *I'm so photogenic!"*

Yes! It works for *everything*. Picture taking, energy levels, health, healing, friendships, money, clarity, inspiration, enlightenment, *EVERYTHING*. Of course, again, for real transformations you'll combine your affirmations with all else we've covered. The truth is, life *is* easy. You *are* a master. You're *of* the Divine. You're here to thrive.

This brings to mind the biblical story of the prodigal child, who turns his back on his father's wealth. He wants to go out into the world and make it on his own, and his father gives him his blessings. In time, however, miserable and broke, he asks his father if he can return, and in an instant his father says yes, plans his son's homecoming party, and the young man's inheritance is fully restored, much to the chagrin of his dutiful brother who never left home.

This metaphorical story is saying in the instant you awaken *to truth*, no matter how far you may have veered from the path in the past, finally understanding deeply who you are and what you can do with your life, *which can be sparked by speaking it first*, your inheritance—more than you could ever spend, ethereally and materially—is fully restored. It takes so little! Know you are unlimited! Know you bring about what you think about! Speak of the transformations you wish to see, as if they already came to pass, and "thy kingdom shall come!"

A Note from the Universe

Question: What do rich folk daydream and visualize about? Answer: Yeah, whatever they want.

Trick question: What do poor folk daydream and visualize about? Answer: Yeah, whatever they want.

You're coming along so quickly,
The Universe

P.S. Whether or not more money is your "thing,"
it works the same no matter who you are: You're free to
think about whatever you want . . . and you'll get it.

I'm aware that many of my little examples center around finan-cial abundance, and it's because the desire for its manifestation is very, very popular, but to state what I trust has been obvious all along, you can substitute abundance in all of these examples for whatever *you* want, including health, peace of mind, and love.

For instance, what do you think happy, fulfilled, successful people daydream and talk about? *Whatever they want!* What do you think sad, lonely, depressed people daydream and talk about? *Whatever they want!* Who doesn't get to think or daydream or speak about whatever they want all day long? We all do. But we've never realized or even been taught about the incredible potency of the words we choose until now. They're more than just words.

YOUR ACTIONS

Pretending changes everything.

We talked about taking action as Step 3 of Playing the Matrix, moving in the general direction of our dreams to the best of our ability, if even down sucky paths. This, here, now, is totally dif-ferent; this section is about playing "make-believe." We're talking about token acts of faith. Little demonstrations, of which I'd like to say there are two types, though the line between them blurs—no problem.

Preparing the Way

The first type of demonstration is about doing something that "prepares the way" for what is implied to be the *inevitable arrival* of your dream. For example, if you were to order furniture tonight, and they said, "Thank you very much! Your new furniture will be delivered this Thursday at 2 P.M." What would you do at home between tonight's ordering it and Thursday at 2 P.M.? Maybe move some or all of the old furniture into a new room, buy complemen-tary throw pillows or a matching rug? *You'd prepare the way—physi-cally—for its inevitable arrival.* You wouldn't go home and worry, *What if it never shows up? What if I don't believe in myself? What if it's not right for me?* No. You ordered it, it's coming, get your home ready to receive it.

With confidence and understanding (again, even if you have to fake either) you should do the same for your "orders" placed with the Universe. Don't worry about it. Or, even if you do worry about it, still prepare the way for its arrival. Maybe you really want the furniture from this hypothetical example, but you can't afford it now. Can you afford the throw pillows? The rug? *Get them!* Start acting like you know the furniture's coming (while you also do what you can, moving in its general direction). Maybe you can gently rearrange some of your existing furniture too. Not that you should vacate the room.

Similarly, considering your priority areas for transformation that you named in earlier chapters, where might you start preparing for the inevitable changes about to sweep through your life? Do you want more friends, to relocate, find a new home, change careers, make more money? Then go! Do stuff that tells your inner witness (your deepest, truest self), "Everything is about to change in fantastic new ways!" This becomes *Limited-Belief-Busting Freebie Tip #4*: how to install new, empowering beliefs (that your life is about to change), without admitting to any limiting ones, simply by acting like it *on a regular basis.*

Some more examples follow, to get you started on making your own lists of make-believe-pretending, which you will follow through on and actually do:

Prepare-the-Way Examples

1. Rearrange the "furniture of your life"—as just reviewed.

2. Shop for and test drive your new car—as if you will soon be buying it.

3. Know interest rates and depositor insurance limits at banks and brokerage firms—you want to be responsible with that avalanche of abundance coming your way!

4. Buy exercise or running shoes—implying that this time you really will take it seriously.

5. Choose a new wardrobe. How are you going to dress once the ship of your dreams comes calling? You don't have to spend a dime on this stuff, yet, but you can window-shop in preparation, and you can fill up online shopping carts to be ready.

Acting "As If"

Alternatively, although similar, instead of preparing for the inevitable arrival of your desired changes, you can deliberately act "as if" they've already happened in your life, probably pretending it was in the very recent past, through simple demonstrations.

Acting "As If" Examples

1. Have a dinner party celebration (with friends who get this stuff). Speak of, celebrate, and toast each other's latest outrageous escapades (your dreams that will be coming true) as if they had already come true.

2. Buy concert tickets for two—particularly if you're desperate and dateless, *as if you were neither.* Oh boy, could I share some stories here, of how women seemed to appear out of thin air after such demonstrations, ironically shifting my issue of loneliness to something else . . .

3. Get a gift for the person you dream of being in your life, as if they already are.

4. If you feel time-starved, take unplanned time off—as if you felt you had more free time. This is a great way to show yourself that you really do have more time than you've probably been complaining about.

5. Write a letter telling someone dear of your latest successes—this is such a favorite of mine, let me elaborate.

Write a Letter Telling Someone Dear of Your Latest Successes

This is not a letter to mail, not yet at least. Consider a long-lost friend or family member and write to them from the perspective of some point in the future, catching up, with great emphasis on present dreams you have for your future, *as if they had already come to pass.*

I suggest making it four parts:

Part 1 – A paragraph or a page to reacquaint. This will be based upon your shared past, true and factual. For example, I'll offer you a hypothetical mini-starter:

> *Hi Roxy, how are you and Tigger? Have you been sailing lately? I really miss our nights out.*

Part 2 – A paragraph or a page on a dream of yours that has "just come true."

> *Guess what! Remember my invention, the kitten leg warmers? The guy who starred in* The Apprentice *just bought the patent. He paid me $7 million. He also asked me out, but I had to fire him.*

Part 3 – Now, this paragraph (or page) is an exercise in and of itself. Explain why "this time" achieving your dream was so easy. Instead of rationalizing why something might not work, as we too often do, I want you to explain why it was such a roaring success. You will be challenged. You're welcome.

> *Ever since I learned to play the Matrix (shameless plug), my life has been easy. I also think it helped that I learned to knit, plus going to the gym, joining Toastmasters, and finishing high school. I've realized I'm a natural born entrepreneur. Oh yeah . . . the Universe goes with me everywhere.*

Part 4 – A paragraph or a page on what you will do next, beyond the dream having come true, with your amazing life.

Anyhow, I'm writing you from Milan. Candy and I just did Italy. Met some guy named Bruno. What a mess! When I get home, I'm going to redecorate and buy you a car. Love, Bambi

P.S. Did you see my pics from Saint-Tropez on TMZ? Suddenly, I'm so photogenic.

Concerning Matters of Grave Importance

Something to consider when playfully pretending with your demonstrations: None of what's been shared here should be in lieu of practical, common-sense conventional approaches to getting what you want, especially in the areas of your health, finances, or anything that might risk the roof over your head. Simply play both ends to the middle. Do the conventional things, like see your normal doctor, financial planner, therapist, coach, or psychiatrist. And then, in addition, try the ideas laid out on these pages. While you could make the theoretical argument that doing the conventional things, like wearing your car seat belt, could be negatively interpreted by your inner witness as a demonstration of your own sensed vulnerability to becoming a traffic statistic, *wear it anyway!*

Any minuscule negativity will automatically be offset by your own natural optimism, especially when you add these suggested empowering demonstrations. There is such leniency and latitude extended to us by life's grace, as I've oft stated, combined with our own profound inclinations to prosper, be healthy, and succeed, that there's no excuse for not covering every base in our march toward dominion over all things—including the negation for the possible existence of limiting, harmful beliefs that we may have.

These token physical demonstrations speak louder than your words, louder than your thoughts. Actually, they *are* your thoughts, but animated. This is still just about your thoughts becoming things. Yet, because you're physically moving with them, they work to suppress any invisible, limiting beliefs that would have otherwise held you back—because clearly, if you are in motion, this speaks louder than any fears that would prefer you were sidelined. Your inner witness says, "Ah, so this *must* be the truth because I see you acting on it." As opposed to seeing you do nothing, which implies, "I'm not worthy. I'm not ready. I'm not good enough. I don't know."

Get a little silly, drive the long way to work, get up at 3 o'clock one morning, stay up until 4 o'clock one night. Shake up your inner witness, show the Universe and yourself that this time things are different, *you're not the same.* And, so, more reasons being given, the floodgates will begin to tremble.

A Note from the Universe

QUESTION: What would you call a world where each challenge bears gifts, your enemies are ancient friends in disguise, and by simply pretending your dreams have already come true, mountains are moved?

ANSWER: Earth.

Too easy?
The Universe

P.S. ANOTHER QUESTION:
What would you call a Being who is as ancient as they are young, as clever as they are innocent, as powerful as they are humble, and who is inevitably destined to live, laugh, and love?
ANSWER: YOU.

GO CRAZY AND HAVE FUN

Getting playful pays big dividends! I've gone a little bit far in sharing this section about my life through its scarier times. Again, I've not done so to talk about me, but to give ideas of stuff to do, or inspire you to make up your own versions of these tools and tricks. And of course, not only have I done all of these, but many, many more. Are some silly and embarrassing? Yes. Is living the life you dream of living worth it? Hell, yes.

1. Write a blueprint for your life.

I first wrote such a blueprint, or script might be a better name, back in 1983, and I still have it. I save most of these things I've done, which allows me to quote them now, verbatim. In this exercise, you'll write down (or I suppose you could draw/paint it if you're so inclined) a narration depicting the amazing, clarifying, and happy events that are soon to unfold in your life. You won't write things like, "I hope" or "I want." Instead, as if you had a blank check to write the future upon, you are to confidently go into future-mode and reminisce by saying things like, "I did" or "I went." Despite such verbiage, the point here is to show yourself how things might go, not how they will go (unless you're general)—there isn't to be any "insistence" that things will go as you write. You'll simply review what you've written from time to time for inspiration, or to charge yourself up before you might visualize the same. You'll find, particularly if you've been feeling low, that this exercise stirs hope and creates possibilities for your future thoughts and manifestations. Here's some of what I wrote that first time, that showed me how I might emerge from the abyss I felt I was in, during the three months in between graduating from college, unemployed with a fancy convertible to pay for, and landing my first degree-related job:

Blueprint. June 8, 1983. Page 1 of 12.

> *The following is a rough draft for the next few years of my life. It is a tentative draft and will be subject to repeat approvals by myself.*
>
> *I am about to be employed by a very reputable firm, it will be a job that will enable me to learn a great deal about the business world and earn a very respectable salary. This job will be a stepping-stone toward great success in the business world (which is right around the corner—in Earth time). Shortly after being with this firm, different ventures will grab my attention, and suddenly I will be keenly aware of the direction I should take. When the time is perfect, I will leap, being confident, excited, and happy all the while, knowing that greatness is ahead of me.*
>
> *Almost instantly good things will happen, I will have backers hounding me, reporters questioning me, and clients buying from me . . .*

Within a month, I got "the" phone call from Price Waterhouse. I give this exercise, and all else I was doing, conventionally and with the woo-woo, credit for that call. But I have to admit, 34 years after writing that blueprint, not once have I ever had backers, reporters, or clients remotely interested in my whereabouts.

There were 11 more pages, each covering different areas of my life that I wanted to bring change to, from romance, to travel, my first home, and the like.

In another blueprint example, but this time from 16 years ago, I wrote:

> *I am a beacon of light, thinker, speaker, healer, and teacher, who touches and enlightens millions of people every day. I am like a spiritual Charles Schultz and my Adventurer's Club (a pseudonym for my website) is my Peanuts strip . . .*
>
> *I am well connected. I love my life. I have fabulous friends. I'm a leader, role model, and the epitome of what I preach—the ultimate life adventurer . . . I live in absolute abundance and harmony . . . My health and mental capacities ever improving.*

*I radiate total well-being . . . wise beyond measure . . . I heal
. . . am youthful . . . Play is a big part of my day . . . I am
pure LOVE.*

This was written before I wrote my first *Note from the Universe*,
which means the first paragraph shared above is rather astounding as the *Notes* have more in common with daily cartoons than
what any of my peers offer, they're what I'm most known for, and
they're still the lifeblood of all else I do.

Also, to anybody who knew me when I wrote this, *I was not
one of those things I claimed to be!* Not outwardly at least, but I was
creating it all, in part through those words, inwardly, where all
manifestations originate.

The truth is, you're also abundant, you're wealthy, you're
healthy, you're eternal. You're all things of the Divine. And should
you ever say, "I'm stupid, I'm poor, I'm overweight . . ." while those
may be tiny, temporary steps on your path, they will never be
who you are. You're lying if you characterize your entire being
this way. Where you are is never who you are. You're unimagin-
ably more. More than the step, more than the path. You are God,
you're rich, you're healthy, you're gorgeous, you're powerful, and
you will be forevermore.

2. Write a letter to the Universe.

I told you it's "God" when I'm scared. But it's "Dear Father
Universe, of whom I am your spiritual, magical son," when I'm
utterly terrified. Of course, you can write such a letter at any time,
not just when you're terrified, but in praise, in gratitude, or when
things are going great.

Dear Father Universe, of whom I am your spiritual, magical son:

*Thank YOU! Thank you for that test, and for instilling me
with the strength, vision, confidence, joy, and love to pass it as I
have! Today is August 1, 2001, and I can hardly believe all that
has happened to me since May 3, 2001! I am FLOORED with*

the remarkable coincidences, the shocking phone calls, the awesome mail (e and snail) that have brought me to this point. My income is skyrocketing, but more importantly, I LOVE all I'm doing and getting set to do! The perfect amount of travel, airports, international destinations, and camaraderie exists, and now floods my life. I love my home, my dogs are very happy, I have plenty of free time . . . And [censored!]. Thank you for my girlfriend(s), thank you for letting Infinite Possibilities *turn out so fabulously, thank you for the contracts, the deals, and the "partners." Thank you for the peace I feel every day. Thank you for the people in my life, thank you for the difference I'm making, and that I'm poised to make, thank you for the fantastically positive cash flow. . . .*

Thank you for Hawaii!

I now see better than ever how I only ever needed to focus on these end results, while turning over the details to you, and this lesson is what I will teach all who will listen. It is so true . . . thoughts become things!!!!

Thank you for my new TV, my new furniture, my cold A/C, the flowers and projects I have going on in my yard, for my vacations, for my friends, for my following, for my girlfriends [second mention, guess it was important to me], [censored], for my inner calm in any storm. . . .

Your friend, Mike, August 1, 2001

There were several other paragraphs, all of the same ilk.

This letter is almost identical to writing a blueprint, but there's a sneaky twist. Can you find it? Why do you think I twice wrote that it was August 1, 2001? Because it wasn't. It was actually May 3, 2001, when I wrote it. But I pretended throughout that I was in the future, removed from the deep rut that had found me on May 3, elevated, recovered, and on top of the world! And from that vantage point, three months in the future (that's how impatient I was), I expressed, "Oh, I get it now! Oh, it was worth it. My life rocks, thanks for everything, including the hard times!"

I'd like to point out that my use of the term *test*, as in "Thank you for that test," gave me a handle on my situation and a more positive way of referring to what I was going through. But please understand that the Universe (God) does not give tests! If there were tests, stuff assigned or administered to us, wouldn't such interfere with our thoughts becoming things? They would. Yet because of old-school views on God and why "He" put us here, people often assume they're being tested, rather than take credit for their sometimes muddled manifestations. Another power robber. It could be said we create our own "tests," not intentionally, but out of confusion. For example, when we "stub our toes" enough, through misunderstanding ourselves and our lives, we will learn, and you could call such experiences "our tests."

> Where you are is never who you are. You're unimaginably more.

3. Write yourself love letters and checks from admirers, friends, and businesses.

As simple as it sounds and for the obvious reasons. In my visualization scrapbook, I used to have a picture of a young woman in a bathing suit that was from a magazine advertisement for a Hawaiian resort. She didn't know it, but we were having a passionate love affair. During the creation of *Infinite Possibilities*, I was promising myself to go to Hawaii as my reward, and preferably with someone like her. Every month, at the completion of each recording, I'd give her a new speech bubble. In one, she said, "Number seven rocks! Let's go to Hawaii!" (That's pretty much the only caption I can share with you.)

Midway through the year, I called up Unity Church of Hawaii in Honolulu, told them of my Unity gigs in Florida, and asked if they needed a guest speaker at the time I was projecting I'd be in Oahu. They hired me . . . for $100. I spoke at their three Sunday morning services, and received my career's first standing ovations. I was soaring. Unfortunately, I took the trip alone. That time.

Similarly, long before I was ever published, I'd write myself letters from publishers, who, as you might imagine, were crazy-happy to have found me and who loved my writings.

Something else I did that anybody with a mortgage can do: I called the provided toll-free number of my lender to get the pay-off amount of my mortgage. *Who calls that number?* I wondered. If they could pay it off, they wouldn't have it, right? I acted as if I could pay mine off. They gave me the exact amount, to the penny, and as a further demonstration, I wrote the check, envelope, and stamped it. I did not mail it—given my account balance, doing so would have been illegal. But I remember feeling, *Yes! I'm going to be that person one day!*

4. Digitally modify images and photos.

I thought the suggested cover Simon & Schuster sent me for *Infinite Possibilities* was a bit lackluster (not really—it just lacked some key elements). So, with some art software, I set out to improve it: "*New York Times* Bestseller! 52 weeks!" I emblazoned across the top. "Seven million copies sold" "As seen on *Oprah* and *Larry King Live*." "Now in 25 languages," which is a number that "coinciden-tally" matches how many foreign languages I'm now published in. "Mike Dooley for President!" Yeah, I got a little carried away. I printed my manipulated cover and plastered it on the walls and doors around my home.

If you're not good with digital manipulation, scissors and glue work just fine.

5. Fill in a mock calendar.

At the turn of the millennium, I was grounded from traveling for low funds and no real reason to go anywhere. So, I took my new year-2000 monthly wall calendar, in which I had not one scheduled date, trip, or event, and I made a bunch up! February 2–4 I'd be in Spain with Dr. Wayne Dyer. February 10–13 I'd be in

Colorado with Dr. Deepak Chopra. February 15–19 I'd be in Seattle with author and channel JZ Knight. I now realize that back then, I only thought I might travel like that on the coattails of somebody super famous. I never imagined that I could do it on my own . . . until I started doing it on my own. All in all, that mock calendar mentioned 24 exotic cities or countries in which I'd be speaking or visiting. To date, I've actually spoken professionally in 17, plus 115 more including Istanbul, Johannesburg, Kuala Lumpur, Moscow, Rome, Reykjavik, and Vienna, to give you an idea; and in many of those cities, I've spoken three or four times.

6. Have pretend talks with family and friends.

This was alluded to in my earlier Chapter 5 challenge of having a dinner party celebration with friends who get this stuff.

Mom, Andy, and I used to do this often, and so later, when something like what we used to pretend really came to pass, they wouldn't believe me.

One morning my website received an e-mail from the Hopkins family's personal assistant, who told me Stella, who loved *The Secret*, would like to communicate with me, if I had time. I had time!! Turns out she was thinking of launching a T-shirt company featuring her husband's doodles. Apparently, Anthony, Hopkins, Sir, is quite the prolific artist between film takes and in back lots. She explained that Anthony also enjoyed *The Secret*, and they both read my biography in the back of the book, which told of my earlier foray into the T-shirt world, selling over one million of them. "Do you still have business contacts in Japan?" was her question, as she rightly knew the Japanese market was a gold mine for popular American T-shirts. Yes! I have a best friend in Japan who distributes U.S. clothing to the entire country! When we wrapped up our communiqué, she said, "Next time you're in LA, Anthony and I would love to have you over to our home for dinner."

"Andy, *you-will-never-guess* who's invited me to dinner?"

"Huh?" he asked, slightly annoyed.

"Hannibal Lecter!!!!"

"Huh!?" He was stupefied, and more annoyed by the seeming charade.

"*Really, Andy!!*" Long silence . . . finally, I let on exactly what had actually transpired so that my excitement would be understood, but by then he must have decided I was just pretending.

Suddenly chipper: "Dude . . . you're late!"

"For what?" I was now stupefied.

"My dinner party!"

"What are you talking about?" I asked.

"Better hurry, Beyoncé and Jay Z just showed up!"

"*No*, Andy . . . my story is real. This is really real. Real real."

Click, he hung up.

7. Scrapbooks and vision boards.

Books and card decks are dedicated to this. Make one, dude! These are awesome tools because they steer your thinking toward end results representing the life of your dreams, or to whatever you make yours represent, automatically bypassing the "cursed hows." And then, those thoughts, when acted upon, will become your things.

8. Overpay your revolving credit, car, and mortgage payments.

Never pay "the minimum," which would be like calling the lender, "Oh, hey GMAC, this is Mike Dooley. I was just wondering . . . what is the absolute least, to the penny, that I could pay this month, without getting in big trouble?" Not the kind of energy you want to put out there on the "plain of manifestation," which is how many authors often refer to living in the jungles of time and space. What would it say about your belief in the avalanches of abundance now rushing toward you? Not much. Instead, here's a trick. Round up to the next dollar. If you owe $352.16, pay $353, *because you're not the kind of person who pays the minimum, ever again.* The day will come when it's not pennies. It'll be dollars, then hundreds of dollars, then tens of thousands. And the day will come when you don't have those kinds of debts anymore. Incidentally, of course, when you overpay these types of debts, the overpayment simply reduces your outstanding principal. It's not throwing money out the window.

A Note from the Universe

If, once upon a time in your life, suddenly and without warning, an event, a person, or some unexpected good news changed everything for the better, it can only mean one thing . . .

Chances are astronomically high that it will happen again.

I'm just sayin'—
The Universe.

EXPEDITED DELIVERY

All of this works because you *are* inclined to succeed with default settings for success and happiness through the roof in every area of your life.

1. Approach creating change as play, not work; as fun, not mandatory.

2. Thinking positive thoughts is never enough; you must act on those thoughts.

3. A tip on legend making: Do what you most want to do and do it your way.

4. Every single challenge of your life bears a gift, "lucky" you.

5. Playing make-believe is the fastest way to believing, and believing is the fastest way to receiving.

TRY THIS AT HOME

Of course, this chapter has been *filled* with exercises I highly recommend you try at home. Now, I'd like to invite you to try part three of the letter-writing exercise we visited.

Take a moment to write down all the reasons any dream you now have *did* come true. Write as a future version of yourself, looking back and telling what made the difference; why *this time* you broke through, rationalizing the great likelihood of everything magically coming together, and naming each such component of your success.

As mentioned, you'll be challenged and forced to see yourself and your situation in a light that heretofore has never existed; from the perspective of having achieved that which you, so far, have not achieved. Do this with pen and paper. Do it now. What is your oldest dream that has not yet come true? If it were to come true in the coming months or year, what would be the main reasons? Why now, when all those years it hadn't? Go there. Imagine being on the other side. This may not be easy, but do it anyway. Fake it. Write down any and every justification you can think of. Here are some ideas to get you started.

1. You've prepared for it, including right up until it manifested (specifically enumerate all you've done and are now doing).

2. You were born worthy.

3. It finally become a greater priority for you.

4. Other areas of your life have been stabilizing.

5. You live in a world where your thoughts become things and your words give you wings.

6. There's enough for everyone—you having yours will not come at anyone's expense.

7. Your positive thoughts are at least 10,000 times more powerful than your negative thoughts, and you're on a roll thinking "the good ones."

8. Your creativity and courage have been snowballing lately.

9. You've been attracting fabulous people into your circle of friends and contacts.

10. You realigned your end results and avoided the Bermuda Triangle of Manifesting.

11. You are a natural born _____ (fill in the blank accordingly).

12. You are by God, of God, for God, and you came here to succeed.

13. Life no longer seems so hectic, you feel peaceful, open, accepting, yet your dreams still move you forward.

14. You are aided by a loving, conspiring Universe with seemingly magical principles.

15. You've read this book and done its exercises (shameless plug).

16. Make this list as long as you can, and be far more specific than I'm able to as I write for everyone, and over time, do versions of this exercise for all of your major dreams.

If making your dreams come true was "easy," would you even care? You wouldn't. It's because they challenge you that you want to live them. Not that it's nearly as hard, or unlikely, as most people would have you believe; compared to old-school thinking, making dreams come true is easy. Still, you'll have to think like you've not thought before, speak like you've not spoken before, and behave like you've not behaved before; break some habits, start new ones, dream bigger, demonstrate, have fun . . . yeah, you so have this.

> All of this works because you *are* inclined to succeed with default settings for success and happiness through the roof in every area of your life.

Chapter 7

THE TIME
OF YOUR LIFE

The best time to plant a tree, another Chinese proverb says, was always 20 years ago, the second-best time is today. This paradigm of seeing old opportunities with new appreciation might hold for the "time of your life." But, do we really need hindsight to see how amazing our lives are today? Why, at university, did my friends and I live for and count the days to each visit home, yet ever since graduation we think of our years at school as among the best of our lives? Why do most people frown at their pictures today, only to see the same photos in a few years and think to themselves, *"Smokin' HOT!"* (unless that's just me)? What if, near the end of our lives, looking back, we suddenly realize that the long and lonely path that strung all our days, months, and years together was neither long nor lonely? That no matter how terrified and timid we felt upon that path, its memories remain so unbearably sweet, they usher forth the happiest of tears? Yeah. We know it's true. We don't have to wait. Which absolutely means, dear reader, that against all seeming odds, this, right now, *today*, as you hold this book in your hands, is the very best time of your life.

Which by no means lowers the bar on your dreams and plans for tomorrow; to the contrary, for all the reasons already mentioned, your joy and celebrations over the present moment, will bring both to bear faster.

In this brief chapter, I'd like to keep you in the here and now, reminding you of a few things you've likely heard before concerning life, dreams, and happiness. The kind of things that none of us can hear often enough. And doing so, help you to have an even better grasp on the value and purpose of our simple Matrix, so that you might sooner rock the living daylights out of the years you have left.

A Note from the Universe

See through the fog that tells others nothing matters, nothing is happening, and effort does not matter.

They realize not, that every second of history . . . was optional.

Burning down the house,
The Universe

P.S. Oh the glory, the sublime glory.

YOU WILL NEVER AGAIN BE AS YOUNG AS YOU ARE TODAY

If you've never heard that adage before and you're younger than 40, it'll probably bring a smile to your face. *Oh . . . wow . . . that's true!* And, whether or not you've heard it before, if you're 40 or older, you're now thinking, *Oh God . . . That's true . . .* The point is, if you've understood what I've been sharing on these pages, in my daily *Notes*, and in all my work, and you could now wish for any one thing, *anything.* One wish. *I know what you'd wish*

> What if, near the end of our lives, looking back, we suddenly realize that the long and lonely path that strung all our days, months, and years together was neither long nor lonely?

for. You'd wish for things to be exactly as they now are, in a world where your thoughts become things, your words give you wings, each day you're pushed onto greatness, all things are possible, and you're an eternal being of light. Does it get any better than that? It doesn't. *Today is as good as it gets in the jungles of time and space.* You might change, which simply means, you might think new thoughts, but the paradise that now surrounds you, that supports you, that allows your thoughts to become things, will not.

CHARITY BEGINS AT HOME, AND THEN BLOOMS LIKE CRAZY

I used to run away from any notion of "serving others," because I thought, from my mildly religious upbringing, that service meant selflessness. I've always understood, if I can't first get myself happy, I'd not be very helpful in helping others be happy. And I still believe that when we learn to shine our own light through following our heart, dreams, and joys, its glow will automatically lighten the darkened paths of others.

It wasn't until a few years ago, however, that I finally learned there's a whole other way of choosing to look at service: Do it because it's fun; because to *you* it's cool; it's what you want to do. Do it because you get a charge from making a difference that will ripple out *forever!*

Do not try to be of service if it's not fun. Or if, for any reason, it's not what *you want to do.* And be on guard for those who help others in the name of sacrifice, selflessness, or altruism, instead of in the name of joy. Because usually, they don't really help that much. Sad is the life that gives without realizing how much, in turn, it receives.

Once ready, and there's no hurry, experiment with this side of random acts of kindness, surprising people and remaining anonymous, or call it "service." It's really fun. Really, really fun. This is what I now call *selfish service.*

YOUR CHALLENGES ARE TAILORED INVITATIONS TO BE EVEN GREATER

As already said, you are more than the step, or even the path, you're on.

Too often, even when reading books like this and agreeing that you're more than your circumstances, that life is beautiful, and that you're poised for greatness, there's a sense of, "Yeah, it's true, I know that, I'm pumped . . . if only I could manifest a huge check in the mail I'd be really happy . . . or if I could undo X, Y, or Z . . . or if I had a partner . . . or if I knew why I was here . . ."

Nope, nada, hold on. You already have every reason, TODAY, to be happy, in spite of your circumstances. Right now.

Additionally, understand that you're not less for your challenges, but more. They're chinks in your armor that *not all that long ago, you did not know you had, or they never would have cropped up!* But by showing up, at long last, for the first time in your entire life, you can address them and move into a higher orbit than you ever knew existed. It means that things are about to get better for you than they have ever been before.

To give you a leg up when challenges arise:

1. Change perspectives, like we did from saying, "I have to do this," to "I get to do this." Similarly, you don't have to deal with your challenges, *you get to.*

2. Beyond changing perspectives, which alone will sometimes be enough to get you smiling, look for the deeper misunderstandings (because they're there) that brought about the wonky circumstances, and their gift will be received.

Don't berate yourself. Don't be critical of yourself. Give yourself every benefit of the doubt. The Divine does. The Divine's still happy. The Divine is still choosing to be you among an infinite number of other choices, evidenced by your mere presence here today. Relish that. Life is fleeting.

You create all you experience and you can re-create that which displeases you, starting today.

A Note from the Universe

One of the most comforting thoughts of all, is knowing that all roads lead "home."

Even more comforting is understanding that you never left.

> *From all of us "back" home,*
> *The Universe*

WHAT ARE YOU WAITING FOR?

What would you like to do, that you could now do, that you aren't doing? Let's do it!

I have too many friends and know of too many acquaintances who have long dreamed of doing things *they can now do*, yet for whatever reason, they're not giving themselves permission to go forth and do it. Know what I mean? Might you be one of those people?

This advice is not meant to stretch your finances or health. Where necessary, scale back and do what's comfortable in the direction of your dreams. Maybe you can't afford the Mediterranean cruise you've dreamed of, but can you afford one closer to home that might also excite you? Maybe you can't go run a marathon, how about a 5K? Maybe you can't visit Japan with a dreamy life partner, yet, but could you go alone?

By doing what you can, with what you have, from where you are, once done, confidence spiked, you'll be emboldened to dream bigger, go farther, take action, and do more.

Start it.

BE HAPPY NOW

Do this, be happy now.

Your happiness is why you chose to be here.

Your happiness is why God wanted to be you.

Your happiness is why you're still here.

There is nothing else, except those "things" now moving you to more happiness. It could fairly and comprehensively be said, that there are only two conditions of the human experience: very happy or about to become very happy. Of course, we must, and can, find happiness in any situation, and we may, rarely, have to redefine "human experience" to include our eternal adventure. But why *wouldn't* we think in such terms, knowing what we now know?! From this day forward, reframe all your thoughts and feelings in terms of truth. Don't let the lure of the illusions trick you. You are bigger. You know better. Happiness now lies under your very nose, thy kingdom has already come, this is what you're here for, let the music play, dance your life away, soon you'll move beyond these illusions, upon which time you'll pine, and long, and dream, of having the exact same chances to be all you can be, that you now have, right here, today.

Just as we contradict ourselves when we dream yet fail to act, so do we contradict ourselves if we state that greater happiness is our goal, yet live sedentary lives. We were not meant to sit around all day, nor were we meant to live without the effect of other people in our lives. Balance is key, but it would always eventually include leaving our homes *and* mingling with people.

Don't let your desire for change go unanswered, nor think that it's the sign of someone who can never be satisfied. This is life's call to be more. It never goes away. It's a divine sense of incompletion, trait of the immortal within us all. I know you've got it, and you're not going to shake it. When *you* realize it's not going away, and that it's how life expands through you, you can then learn to be happy despite it. As opposed to "Well, once I feel a little better about myself, and I have a faster car, and I do the other thing . . . then I'll give myself permission to be happy." You were born with permission to be happy. You already have abundant reasons. Your life on Earth is the victory lap you earned prior to your arrival in these jungles. Be happy now and all else will be added unto you.

THE TIME OF YOUR LIFE

1. This is it, right here, right now, as good as it's going to get.

2. Practice the art of selfish service.

3. Your life is awesome, in part, because of your present challenges.

4. The secret to living the life of your dreams is to indulge now to any degree you can.

5. Happiness does not mean you've settled for less; it signals you're ready for more.

A Note from the Universe

I distinctly remember the conversation. We were having triple-chocolate brownie fudgesicles, listening to Beethoven's "Fifth" before he even was Beethoven, overlooking the galaxy, when you mentioned how neat you thought it would be to one day have dreams you didn't know you'd inevitably manifest, to have challenges you didn't know you'd inevitably conquer, and to have friends you didn't know you'd inevitably meet.

And as I leaned forward in total awe, all agog, wanting to learn more of your genius and courage, I almost fainted when you added, "And should it ever appear as if I could use your help, before I even begin helping myself, back off or you'll ruin everything."

You memory-maker you,
The Universe

P.S. Or were we listening to DJ Khaled's "We Takin' Over,"
before he even was DJ Khaled?

The wording is tricky in that *Note*, but I doubt there's a better way to capture the nature of our choice to be here in these hallowed jungles of time and space, where all is supremely well. In some greater reality, our deeper selves are now gently being rocked by ancient friends in some hammock. Snoring and drooling in a greater sleep, we're dreaming of being who we now are, for having dared to live on the razor's edge of reality creation, as creators, yet hiding this from ourselves to make this the greatest adventure ever devised by Divine Mind.

In this dream, we think we are this guy or that girl, believing in the trusty "lies" of have versus have not, here versus there, and now versus then. The very illusions that make possible this adventure. Because if you "have not" and you want to "have," are "here" but wish to be "there," live "now" but want to move forward, again, *game on!* Because of this voluntary entrapment, the adventure begins. Moving through the affairs of your life. Falling in love. Being loved. Scared, excited, happy, sad, and unbeknownst to you, totally writing the script every single day. At least until now. And this, your Creator-Hood, is what you wanted to discover anew. Because you can. Because you love. Because you're a forever being. This is the nature of your choice.

The truth, the condition upon which you ventured forth, was that you are everywhere, always at once; that you are the sun, the moon, and the stars; a "love being" in the illusions of time and space.

> It could fairly and comprehensively be said, that there are only two conditions of the human experience: very happy or about to become very happy.

In the blink of an eye you're going to be back in the palm of God's hand, and then you're going to wake up and you're going to be like, "That was *so* real. I thought I was {FirstName} {LastName}. I thought I was *here* and then I was *there*. I thought I could do *this* and I couldn't do *that* . . . Let's go back! Let's go do it again . . . we'll be best friends, remind each other of who we really are . . . and read Hay House books! Let's go back to that beautiful dream of that opulent, abundant paradise, otherwise known as Earth . . . ."

TRY THIS AT HOME

What would you like to do, that you could now do . . . that you aren't doing? Let's do it!

My small team in Orlando helped me come up with these three columns. These're not meant to be bucket list items. Those are different. Those are things you cannot now do, but you dream of doing someday before your life is over. This is a different list. These are things that you could now do but for whatever reasons, they're not on your calendar. What's up with that? Why would that be if you've always thought one day you'd do them, you can now do them, but aren't? Are you waiting to meet that special someone? Perhaps you'll meet them doing one of these things. Perhaps you'll come into your abundance once you get out and start indulging in your dreams today, to any degree you can. Not only will you enjoy doing these things, but you'll set the stage for further growth by doing them, and because of that, more dreams coming true in the future.

To stir your memory, please consider actually putting the relevant items on the lists below on your calendar, and commit. For the likely things we did not think of, but that are personal wishes of your own, for which we've left space below, book them too.

✓ Take a cruise

✓ Rent a convertible

✓ Become big bro/
  big sister

✓ Learn to paint

✓ Take up golf

✓ Volunteer

✓ Learn gardening

✓ Redecorate home

✓ Write poetry

✓ Buy a home

✓ Buy second home

✓ Parachute

✓ Travel
  around the world

✓ Purchase
  new wardrobe

✓ Go on a
  shopping *spree*!

✓ Throw a party

✓ Vacation alone

✓ All-day
  spa treatment

✓ Go on an
African safari

✓ Join a book club

✓ Sleep
overnight at beach

✓ Wake up one
hour earlier

✓ Write a book

✓ Meditate/visualize

✓ Travel
internationally

✓ Eat dinner out more

✓ Join a dating website

✓ Take dance classes

✓ Visit your
local theater

✓ Learn to belly dance

✓ Relax/sleep in more

✓ Join a club, any club

✓ Go on a
TUT WOW tour

✓ Have more three-
day weekends

✓ Visit the
Greek islands

✓ Learn to give
pro massage

✓ Send flowers
for no reason

✓ Make amends
/ apologize

✓ Study astronomy

✓ Sponsor a
child overseas

✓ Watch the sunrise

✓ Ride hot-air balloon

✓ Buy new car

✓ Buy your dream car

✓ Dress to
(really) impress

✓ Give a gift to
a stranger

✓ Burn candles/incense

✓ Go back to school

✓ Design a
T-shirt to sell

✓ Join Toastmasters

✓ Learn a language

✓ Go to
airport w/out tix

✓ Take cooking class

✓ Read more books

✓ Write
your biography

✓ Learn to sail

✓ Learn to scuba dive

✓ Learn to fly a plane

✓ Open
investing account

✓ Study photography

✓ Buy a hot tub

✓ Adopt a child or pet

✓ See a
Broadway musical

✓ Buy a motorcycle

✓ Join local
sports team

✓ Buy season tickets

✓ Run for an office

✓ Ask for a raise

✓ Start a nonprofit org

✓ Babysit for a friend

✓ Read to a child

✓ Buy a tablet

✓ Forgive a
debt/grudge

✓ Move to a new town

On the lines below, write down at least four more personal dreams that you can already BEGIN planning or doing, and *do 'em!*

1._____

2._____

3._____

4._____

A Note from the Universe

Before this odyssey ever began, there was you, your best friends, and wide-eyed curiosity among you about who would be the first to leap, the first to forget, the first to kiss, the first to tell, the first to fall, the first to get back up, and the first to remember that it all began with a dare:

To love in spite of it all.

Is that you, Mergatroid?
The Universe

P.S. I remember the glint in your eyes . . . all three of them.

ACKNOWLEDGMENTS

In gratitude to the entire Hay House family, from its readers to its leaders and the team in between—especially to Anne Barthel, Patty Gift, and Reid Tracy. The freedom you give me, the faith you show, and the kinship you share are more than I ever thought might exist between an author and a publisher.

ABOUT THE AUTHOR

Mike Dooley is an international tax consultant turned entre-preneur turned writer for "The Universe." He's the founder of a philosophical Adventurers Club on the Internet that's now home to over 750,000 members from around the world. His inspira-tional books emphasizing spiritual accountability have been pub-lished in 25 languages, and he was one of the featured teachers in the international phenomenon *The Secret*. Mike is the author of Hay House's *Life on Earth, From Deep Space with Love,* and *The Top Ten Things Dead People Want to Tell You*; he is also known for his free *Notes from the Universe* e-mailings and his *New York Times* bestsellers *Infinite Possibilities* and *Leveraging the Universe*. He speaks worldwide on life, dreams, and happiness. You can find Mike at his website: www.tut.com.

HAY HOUSE TITLES OF RELATED INTEREST

YOU CAN HEAL YOUR LIFE, the movie,
starring Louise Hay & Friends
(available as a 1-DVD program, an expanded 2-DVD set,
and an online streaming video)
Learn more at: www.hayhouse.com/louise-movie

THE SHIFT, the movie,
starring Dr. Wayne W. Dyer
(available as a 1-DVD program, an expanded 2-DVD set,
and an online streaming video)
Learn more at: www.hayhouse.com/the-shift-movie

*E-CUBED: Nine More Energy Experiments That Prove Manifesting
Magic and Miracles Is Your Full-Time Gig,* by Pam Grout

LIFE'S OPERATING MANUAL: With the Fear and Truth Dialogues,
by Tom Shadyac

RESILIENCE FROM THE HEART: The Power to Thrive in Life's Extremes,
by Gregg Braden

THE UNIVERSE HAS YOUR BACK: Transform Fear to Faith,
by Gabrielle Bernstein

All of the above are available at your local bookstore,
or may be ordered by contacting Hay House (see next page).

We hope you enjoyed this Hay House book. If you'd like to receive our online catalog featuring additional information on Hay House books and products, or if you'd like to find out more about the Hay Foundation, please contact:

Hay House, Inc., P.O. Box 5100, Carlsbad, CA 92018-5100
(760) 431-7695 or (800) 654-5126
(760) 431-6948 (fax) or (800) 650-5115 (fax)
www.hayhouse.com® • www.hayfoundation.org

Published and distributed in Australia by:
Hay House Australia Pty. Ltd., 18/36 Ralph St., Alexandria NSW 2015
Phone: 612-9669-4299 • *Fax:* 612-9669-4144 • www.hayhouse.com.au

Published and distributed in the United Kingdom by:
Hay House UK, Ltd., Astley House, 33 Notting Hill Gate, London W11 3JQ
Phone: 44-20-3675-2450 • *Fax:* 44-20-3675-2451 • www.hayhouse.co.uk

Published and distributed in the Republic of South Africa by:
Hay House SA (Pty), Ltd., P.O. Box 990, Witkoppen 2068
info@hayhouse.co.za • www.hayhouse.co.za

Published in India by: Hay House Publishers India,
Muskaan Complex, Plot No. 3, B-2, Vasant Kunj, New Delhi 110 070
Phone: 91-11-4176-1620 • *Fax:* 91-11-4176-1630 • www.hayhouse.co.in

Distributed in Canada by:
Raincoast Books, 2440 Viking Way, Richmond, B.C. V6V 1N2
Phone: 1-800-663-5714 • *Fax:* 1-800-565-3770 • www.raincoast.com

Access New Knowledge.
Anytime. Anywhere.

Learn and evolve at your own pace
with the world's leading experts.

www.hayhouseU.com